the
Dream
Oracle

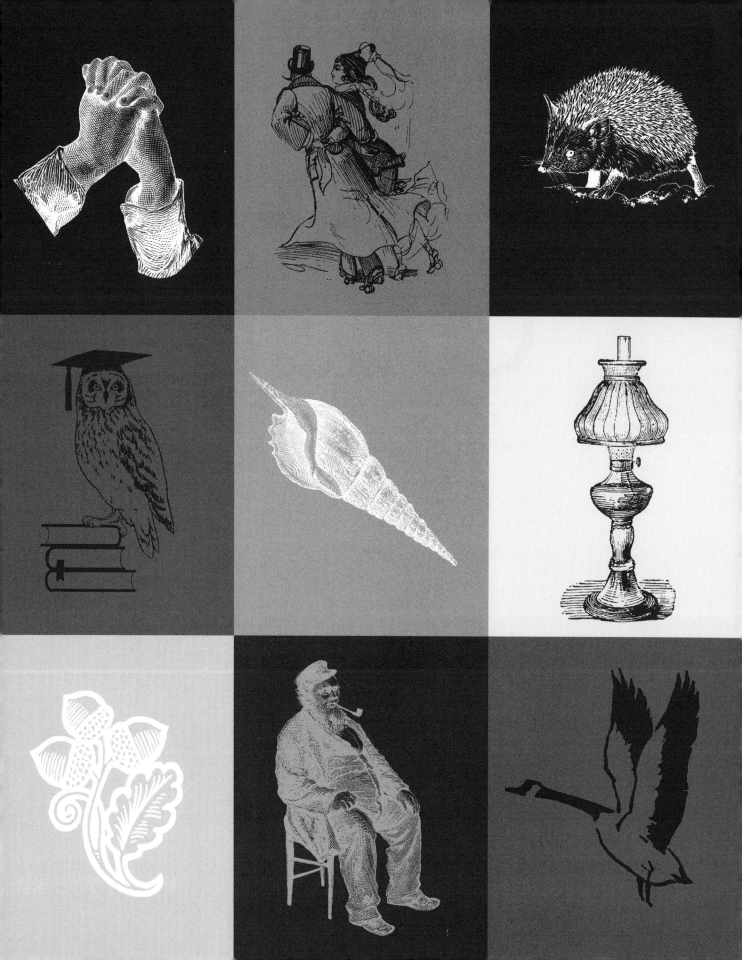

the Dream Oracle

Discover your hidden depths through
symbolism and the Tarot

PAMELA BALL

ARCTURUS

PICTURE CREDITS

ARCTURUS

This edition published in 2011 by Arcturus Publishing Limited
26/27 Bickels Yard, 151–153 Bermondsey Street,
London SE1 3HA

Copyright © 2011 Arcturus Publishing Limited/Pamela Ball

ISBN: 978-1-84837-940-4
AD001862EN

Printed in Singapore

CONTENTS

INTRODUCTION

Almost inevitably when we begin to take an interest in either dreams or the Tarot, we will very soon become aware of the startling similarities they share. This book sets out to explore those similarities and to elucidate how we can use their common imagery to give us greater understanding of ourselves and our life Journey. We can do this by using them to access, and to control, our own Dream Oracle, that inner guru or teacher we all possess.

The word oracle in its original form meant 'wise counsel', and our Dream Oracle can provide us with such counsel. Our dreams are uniquely our own, a reflection of our deep subconscious. If we learn to listen, hear and evaluate the information they are trying to impart, it can only be to our benefit.

One way of evaluating our dreams is to compare them with the rich imagery of the Collective Unconscious and what is now known as depth psychology, or access to the inner psyche. The psyche is what was known to the Ancient Greeks as the animating principle, and refers to the forces in us all that influence thought, personality and behaviour – those aspects of ourselves which make us truly individual. So the idea of a system or book which combines more than one way of accessing such archetypal images, those 'pictures' of universal experience that are imprinted within each of us, has a great deal of merit.

It is these images that are shared by both our dreams and by the Tarot, and indeed by myth and fairytale alike. Thus, an imp-like figure will evoke the same response in us whether it appears in Tarot, as it does in the card of the Devil, or in our dreams as a mischievous irritation. When we learn to contrast and compare the two systems through the use of dream manipulation and meditation, we open up a whole new world. Thus our Dream Oracle becomes a manual for translation between what initially seem to be two different languages.

Our first consideration in the book is the Tarot. Tarot means 'truth', and though nobody quite knows where the cards truly originated, it is now widely accepted that they were probably used by the Knights Templar and disseminated throughout Europe by the Romany gypsies. The earliest known cards date back to the 15th century and were hand-painted. With the invention of the printing press, they became much more readily available, and unfortunately degenerated into something of a parlour game.

In fact, they have always touched on some basic truths, as they picture the stages of growth from youth and innocence towards maturity. This has become known as the Fool's, or Innocent's, Journey. The Fool (and we with him) starts out with little but his enthusiasm for life and finishes up a wiser – and more able – being who is ready to help others on their way. It parallels what is known as the Hero's Journey, the monomyth or basic story, of the path to spiritual awareness.

The Tarot pack of 78 cards is divided into two parts – the Major Arcana (defined as 'hidden things') and the Minor. The Major Arcana consists of 22 representations of the stages of growth towards understanding our own truth: the Fool's Journey. The Minor Arcana depicts – in a set of four suits from which our modern playing cards are derived – the four different aspects of life we come across in the everyday: finance, love, work and difficulties. In *The Dream Oracle*, we have described the imagery of each card in the Major Arcana and given explanations of their significance, and also examined their associations and secondary images. A resumé of the key features of each card makes a useful quick reference. For the Minor Arcana, we have outlined both the main and subsidiary associations of the four suits, the court cards and the number cards.

The second section of the book explores the subject of Dream Management, which could be considered to be the bridge between Tarot and dreams. It has often been said that the mind is a poor servant,

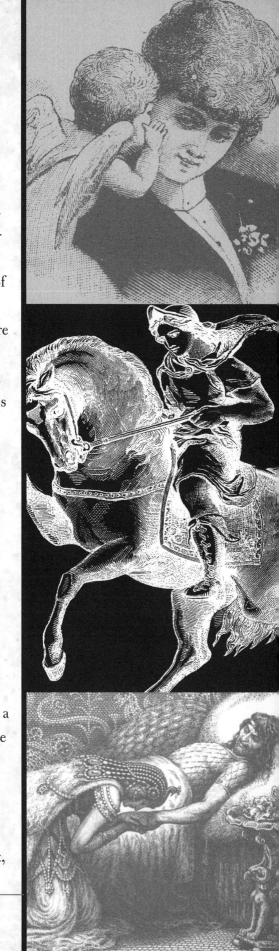

but in our view it makes an able ally. For us to make sense of our inner Dream Oracle, we must learn to focus on every aspect of our dreams and to be able to understand the randomness of both the imagery and the way that it is presented.

Focused daydreaming, creative visualization and meditation are all techniques which, once we understand how to use them, help us to 'zoom in' to what is essential and what is not. Harnessing the daydreaming mind as it idles, creating ideal scenarios through visualization, meditating on the outcome and learning to manipulate that outcome are all invaluable in the conscious understanding of the Dream Oracle. When we then use the Tarot as a backdrop, it enhances our understanding and allows us to take more control of our lives.

Conversely, by employing the system in reverse order – focusing on Tarot images that are relevant to us, meditating on them, using creative visualization followed by focused daydreaming – we can enhance our dream content. We can then begin to make use of dreams to make changes in the way we operate in the everyday world. We trust our inner Dream Oracle enough to allow it to direct our lives.

The third and largest section of the book considers dreams and dreaming. For ease of interpretation it broadly follows the classification of dream content used by Calvin Hall and Robert van de Castle in their quantitative analysis of dreams in the mid-20th century. Interpretations of images are given within these broad frameworks:

The participation of the dreamer – the Fool's Journey from innocence to maturity.

Settings and scenery – places and environments, buildings and structures, nature, ecology and plants, obstructions and obstacles, water, weather and time.

Characters and participants – people, family, animals, birds, insects, and mythological, magical and spiritual characters.

Interactions, qualities and principles – behaviour, actions and activity, occupations, belief systems, the body, and clothes and appearance.

Emotions, reactions and responses – positive interactions and celebrations, negative actions and interactions, relationships and intimacy.

Integral objects – furniture, food and drink, symbolic imagery.

Transitional elements – methods of transport and types of journey.

And then I woke up . . . – endings and conclusions

As an author, it has been fascinating to be able to draw comparisons between the Fool's Journey, the Hero's Journey and the Dreamer's Journey and to realize how closely aligned they are. We explore this much more comprehensively in the section entitled The Dreamer, The Hero and The Fool.

Our interpretations of dream images are of the better known and more frequently occurring ones. It may take a little thought for you to tease out the meanings for your own individual dream images. However, our interpretations will give you the right directions to follow so that you can find the meanings that are unique to you. Eventually you will learn to be more specific in your interpretation as you yourself become more proficient at understanding your personal Dream Oracle's language. In fact, your Dream Oracle may well help you; interestingly, the dreaming mind will often present alternative images if the initial ones are not well understood. The concept can even be reviewed and refined until the conscious mind has the 'aha' experience and accepts what is being suggested. It is this experience, or sense of revelation, which makes interpretation of dreams so fascinating.

In the example dreams we have given – a series of templates, if you like, for your dream interpretation – we have used each part of the book in slightly different ways to unravel deeper and deeper relevance and show how to apply the findings in daily life.

The wonderfully evocative illustrations of the Tarot ably describe the basic route of Life's Journey; the Dream Management section shows how to use the map; and our Dream Oracle is, in effect, our inner satellite navigation system.

We trust you will both enjoy, and learn from, your personal Journey.

TAROT:
THE KEY TO OUR DREAMS

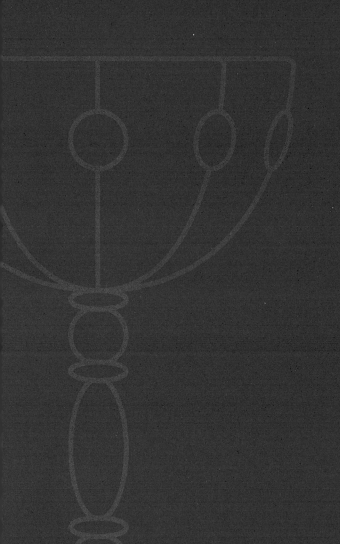

The symbolism we encounter in our dreams taps into a rich source of common imagery drawn from shared experiences of culture, stories, myths and spiritual or religious references – a universal collection of images that have become archetypal representations of people, situations, problems or achievements. When we strive to interpret what our dreams are trying to communicate to us, we automatically draw on the symbolism of these images in our attempts to find enlightenment.

Even dreaming creatively, however, can fail to give us all the information we need to adequately explain the images and symbols that present themselves to us when we are sleeping. But research has highlighted the remarkable similarity of dream imagery with the symbolism of the Major and Minor Arcana of the Tarot. Part of the mystique of the Tarot is that it can be used in so many ways, not just in its currently most recognizable form as a divinatory tool. Therefore if we learn about these images through Tarot, we can transfer the knowledge we develop to our dream interpretation in order to give us the clarity we seek, which will allow us to personalize our dream experiences in a way that perhaps no other psychological investigation can. By combining Tarot with dream interpretation, we can develop complementary methods of understanding that can be of immeasurable benefit on our life Journey.

In this section we shall explore the significant imagery of the Tarot. As you work through the book, you will discover how it can be used to give you a deeper understanding of your dream experiences. This imagery is simple to interpret and invaluable as a tool to work with in enhancing the content of your dreams.

MAJOR ARCANA

The Major Arcana in its entirety leads us securely along the path of life's journey of self-development – the Journey of Life – sometimes called the Hero's Journey or the Fool's Journey. Like us, the Fool sets out full of hope, encountering obstacles, challenges and triumphs along the way. In the Major Arcana, each card marks a particular stage on this journey, representing – in multi-layered imagery – specific personalities, circumstances and issues that we all encounter on our individual Journey of Life.

The first card in the Major Arcana represents the Fool himself. As we study each subsequent card, we see that it marks a particular point on the Fool's own journey where, in all innocence, he comes to a realization of a particular quality or transitional stage. We accompany him on his journey as we acclimatize ourselves to the image on the card, and the significance of the main figure or idea.

Familiarity with each image, and the ideas embodied by it, will help us to develop the insights that are necessary to a full understanding of where we are in our lives. The primary images are the crucial ones, but there are myriad symbols in the cards that, while perhaps not all as important, also yield crucial information relevant to our deeper selves. In some cases, an astrological sign or planet has not been ascribed; this is because we have followed as closely as we can the more mystical correspondences of esoteric teaching and no such correspondence has as yet been made. While we have chiefly used the Roman pantheon of gods and goddesses, we have also included others from different systems of belief, where appropriate. Your own interests might lead to some further fascinating research.

The assimilation of the information gleaned from the images will help you develop to the point where – along with the Fool or Hero – you understand the world, your place in it and how you can bring stability into that world.

MINOR ARCANA

The Minor Arcana is divided into four suits and delineates the more down-to-earth joys, challenges and difficulties an individual may meet along the way. Spanning, as the Minor Arcana suits do, the practical, emotional, mental and personal growth aspects of everyday life and their esoteric elements, their symbolism is particularly timeless and is often seen in modern dreams. Each of the four suits – Pentacles, Cups, Wands and Swords – has ten numbered cards and four court cards: a king, a queen, a knight and a page. In some packs, a princess replaces the knight. In many ways, these personalities form a link between the Major Arcana and the numbered cards in the suits, with their more down-to-earth, everyday occurrences.

As we shall see later, our Dream Oracle has the propensity to draw on the rich imagery of bygone ages, connecting us with myth and fairytale, and allowing us to maintain an objectivity we might not otherwise achieve. The personalities of the court cards resonate with our ability to create our own inner story.

TAROT PACKS

There was a huge upsurge in the study of all things esoteric – including Tarot – at the beginning of the 20th century. Pamela Coleman Smith was commissioned to design a set of Tarot cards for Arthur Edward Waite, a mystic, scholar and member of the Hermetic Order of the Golden Dawn. Her intuitive interpretations and use of symbolism have become the basis for many of the modern Tarot packs.

The Tarot images we show in this book are based on those created for the Rider Waite pack, occasionally known as the Waite-Smith pack. We have illustrated only the Major Arcana, although we do briefly explain the Minor Arcana. Simple and unambiguous, the illustrations are ideal for anyone new to Tarot and the method of dream interpretation we explore in this book because they are simple to interpret, and first class as tools to work with in enhancing your understanding of your dream content.

For more experienced users of Tarot, who prefer to use other packs, the symbolism should still be evident. Whether the Tarot pack is mythical, humorous, mathematical or highly mysterious, on some level or another it will resonate with our inner being and will tap into our own rich store of archetypal imagery – the stuff that dreams are made on.

TAROT AND YOUR DREAMS

When we become aware of our internal Dream Oracle, that part of us which has an awareness beyond the ordinary, there is a kind of two-way traffic set up. It is as though there is a dialogue created between the inner, more private self and the outer – the one that operates in the everyday world. These two parts of us, rather than being in conflict with one another, begin to co-operate; when they work in harmony, things begin to happen in the exterior world in a quite magical way.

There are times when we need a trigger which will awaken those innate abilities to understand ourselves. Tarot provides that external stimulus and dreams the internal explanation. Working on the principle that combining two things creates four times the power, we thus have a very powerful tool, which works both ways, showing us meaning in our dreams, and offering us a method by which we can stimulate dreams for further elucidation. The relationship between dream imagery and Tarot imagery – sharing, as they do, archetypal representations and symbolism – means their interaction provides us with the most insightful of tools to psychological understanding.

Even without any particular specialist knowledge of the meaning of Tarot, the images will tap into our inner wisdom and allow our dreams to speak more fully to us. With the help of this book, you will learn to marry the impressions and interpretations from both dream and Tarot and truly become a personal Dream Oracle or 'wise pronouncement'.

We do not need to treat the representations as divinatory tools in themselves but more as a way of clarifying our own dreamscapes. Therefore, though traditionally the cards have different meanings when reversed, it is not necessary to deal with this potentially more negative interpretation at this stage.

MEDITATION

Simple contemplation of the Tarot can be very rewarding in a number of ways. Deeper meditation on the illustrations or the cards gives a depth of understanding and perception that it is probably not possible to achieve in any other way. Such deliberation can be done with each illustration so that your overall understanding becomes quite phenomenal. Ideally such meditation should be done before you go to sleep. You might then decide to sleep with your chosen illustration or card under your pillow to help enhance your dreams.

TAROT MEDITATION

To meditate more fully on the Tarot you will need the Major Arcana of your chosen pack and a quiet place free from interruptions. These simple instructions will help you to maximize the information available to you.

- Form a circle of the cards in numbered order, placing the Fool in the centre. This is both your starting and your finishing point.
- Study the main image of the Fool carefully. Recognize that this represents you as you set out on your journey of discovery.
- Imagine or visualize yourself as the Fool and really feel him as he is, carefree and fancy-free.
- Next look carefully at the secondary images on the card and try to sense how they relate to the main figure. What use would you make of them? How would there be an interaction between any of them?
- If you are able to, try to become each image in turn. Do not be too disappointed if this is difficult to begin with; with practice it becomes easier.
- Now return to the main figure and sense yourself as the Fool within the landscape. See everything through his eyes very clearly with a fresh sense of wonder (at this point, like Alice through the looking glass, you may well have transcended your everyday reality).
- If you can, spend a few moments in this state – one that is almost dream-like – before returning to reality and reorientating yourself in the everyday.
- Finally, see how each card applies to your own life at this particular point.
- Choose a new card every time you wish to learn more about the stages of the Fool's progress towards maturity and follow the same procedure with each card.

As you master the Major Arcana, your dream symbolism will often take on a deeper meaning and allow for greater understanding. Then, using the various techniques introduced in the Dream Management section, you can enhance your link with your own internal Dream Oracle.

THE FOOL

Which then was wisdom and which was folly?
The fool, as I think, at the chasm's brink
Did, even as I, in the end rejoice.

Arthur Edward Waite (1857–1942)

THE IMAGE

In the majority of Tarot packs, the Fool is not a numbered card as such, but is given the cipher 0. This is to signify the beginning of creativity or the point of nothing (lack of form or the absence of any thing). In classic Tarot packs he is shown almost invariably accompanied by a dog and carrying a bundle or knapsack on a branch or wand on one shoulder. He stands at the edge of a precipice, his eyes turned towards the sky. The sun shines down on him and the cold mountains are in the distance.

THE SIGNIFICANCE

The Fool in the Tarot has two significances. At the beginning of the Journey of Life he represents the innocence of youth, a devil-may-care attitude and a lust for life that will take him far. He faces a future full of promise, and carries with him all that is necessary for the first part of his journey. He seems to be unaware of the dangers which might beset him and oblivious to any warnings.

The negative aspects of the card reveal folly and sheer exuberance and, if misused, a lack of structure. His lack of attention to detail, shown by his ignorance of the drop below, can become a predicament.

The second significance arises at the end of his journey when he becomes the 'Holy Fool'. He has overcome the obstacles that have been set for him; his focus is on the sky, towards his heaven; he has no fear of the chasm beneath him because he knows that if he falls, he can fly. He has tested his faith in himself – along with the loyalty of his faithful companion – and has pared down his burdens to the bare necessities that will take him to the next phase of his existence.

ASSOCIATIONS AND SECONDARY IMAGES

Almost invariably, the main association with the Fool is with freedom, so the associated gods are those slightly wild, unregulated ones. In Greek and Roman mythology these are Dionysus and Bacchus respectively, the god who gifted both wine and ecstasy to

humanity. The pagan god is Pan, while in Hindu mythology the goddess would be Kali as she dances, before her transformation into Parvati. The card is ruled by Uranus, known as the planet of sudden opportunities.

BRANCH OR WAND This image both represents and forecasts growth and attainment in the natural or magical arts. Our traveller must learn to live within the physical realm and take advantage of what is to hand to help him on his Journey.

CAP AND FEATHER In Tarot, the headgear a character wears is significant. The feather – which does not droop – in our Fool's cap represents the soul, willing obedience and optimism.

DOG The crucial image of the dog represents a loyal, faithful and protective companion. Alert, sometimes he encourages and other times he warns of danger. He is often thought to represent divine wisdom.

KNAPSACK The Fool has not yet burdened himself with non-essentials and takes only what he can carry as easily as possible. He trusts that he will find everything he needs along the way. The knapsack that he carries is sometimes thought to contain those lessons that he must learn on this part of his Journey of Life.

MOUNTAINS These are often shown as cold and inhospitable – an alien world. In this environment the Fool must learn to survive by his wits alone. He must learn to take note of his surroundings and to become aware of danger.

SUN According to our own level of understanding, the Sun in the card of the Fool signifies either the ultimate goal we can reach or a nurturing, all-powerful source of energy.

KEY FEATURES

ELEMENT Air.

PLANET Uranus.

NUMEROLOGY This card is designated as the cipher 0 or zero, which come from the Arabic *safira* meaning 'it was empty'. It represents the circle of the universe and the mathematical beginning point.

DEITIES Dionysus/Bacchus, Kali, Pan.

KEY WORDS Innocence. Potentiality. Spirituality. The beginning and the end.

RELATED CONCEPTS Intellect and the powers of the mind. The path of life, the way forward. New ventures, fresh creativity, stepping forward into the unknown.

THE MAGICIAN

Remember today, for it is the beginning of always.
Today marks the start of a brave new future filled with
all your dreams can hold. Think truly to the future and
make those dreams come true.

Unattributed

THE IMAGE

Assigned the number 1, the Magician is the first stage of development in the Journey of Life, that is pictured in the Major Arcana. He is usually shown with a collection of tools set out in front of him, of which he is fully aware. These are often represented by the objects associated with the four suits of the Minor Arcana: a wand or stave, a cup, a pentacle or coin, and a sword. They all signify the practicalities of life and how they might be used to help the Magician learn his craft. He gestures with one hand towards the heavens and with the other towards the Earth.

Above his head, or depicted in his hat, is the sign of infinity, suggesting that he must apply intellect to be able to use his power successfully. He usually wears a girdle around his waist and either carries a light or is depicted bathed in, or using, light in a particularly magical way. Where flowers are shown they are most often depicted as the rose and perhaps also the lily.

THE SIGNIFICANCE

At this stage of his journey our traveller has become the Magician. To use magic and to be able to control the energies that doing so entails, the Magician must know and understand the tools he uses. From an overall perspective, his gestures indicate that he understands the idea of manifestation – 'as above, so below'.

The power that he has access to, particularly through the double-ended source of light he carries in his hand, must be grounded before it can be used properly. He himself must act as transformer. He must 'step down' or regulate the power so it becomes more accessible both to himself and others. Only then can he use the practical tools at his disposal. Some he will use more easily than others.

ASSOCIATIONS AND SECONDARY IMAGES

The Magician's primary association is Adam as the first man, formed from the Divine Logos and inhabiting a world that is rich in potential. He is also Hermes

or Mercury, the classical messenger of the gods, not quite with his feet on the ground and therefore sometimes likely to forget his own origins. His knowledge is that of instinct, not book learning. His planetary association is also with Mercury.

CANDLE/LIGHT SOURCE The source of light that the Magician holds represents the illumination of knowledge or enlightenment, without which he cannot work.

FLOWERS Roses have been identified with love and passion since the times of the Ancient Greeks and Romans, particularly with the goddesses Aphrodite and Venus, and also the Egyptian goddess Isis.

GIRDLE The girdle is a symbol of special wisdom, containment and protection. Often plaited and knotted, it signifies balance between body, mind and spirit. It can also suggest that the wearer belongs to a particularly gifted or honoured group of people.

SIGN OF INFINITY The sign of infinity above the Magician's hat represents the perfect balance between any two polarities. Out of that balance arises the potential for incredible power and knowledge.

TABLE The Magician is frequently shown standing at a table, which most often has four legs. This symbolizes his connection with the mundane world; he needs the tools to access the higher knowledge. By offering these tools to be consecrated he turns the table into an altar, a portal into the sacred realms.

TOOLS The tools on the table are those he must learn to use before he can continue on his journey. Wands represent growth, creativity and pure potential. Swords are said to represent challenges or difficulties. Tarot Cups are related to our emotions, our hearts and inner being. The Tarot Pentacle is associated with what might be called practical magical dreaming and manifestation.

KEY FEATURES

ELEMENT All.

PLANET Mercury.

NUMEROLOGY This card is designated 1, signifying unity, self-actualization and personal potential.

DEITIES Hermes/Mercury.

KEY WORDS Direction. Skill. Organization of thought. Wisdom. Invocation. Magic.

RELATED CONCEPTS Divine Logos. Adam, the first man. The act of experience and conscious direction of energy. Occult power.

THE HIGH PRIESTESS

Wonder is the beginning of wisdom.

Greek proverb

THE IMAGE

Assigned the number 2, the somewhat cold and aloof High Priestess – a young woman – sits on a throne in front of two pillars, often with the letter B inscribed on the left, black one and the letter J on the right, white one. She is richly dressed in a cloak, thus highlighting her purity. This partially hides the scroll she carries, often labelled *Tora*, meaning truth. Her horned headdress shows her allegiance to the Moon, as does the crescent Moon at her feet. The cross on her chest has equal arms, signifying that she works in reflected light that brings light into darkness. Behind her is a veil imprinted with palm trees and pomegranates. Seated facing us, she is not prepared to reveal what is hidden unless she finds us worthy.

THE SIGNIFICANCE

The High Priestess is sometimes shown as the female pope. Opinions vary as to when this depiction changed from showing her as the head of a Church to representing her as the feminine intrinsic link to the Divine with her own intuitive abilities. When we also take into account that pre-Christian, pagan matriarchal religions in places like Sumeria considered their high priestesses more important than their high priests, this suggests a return to old beliefs. Meeting her, our traveller must recognize the duality in her, and through her learn to use his own intuition without fear. He must understand that she guards her truth carefully and uses her powers subjectively, rather than with the brashness of objectivity, to decide who is a worthy recipient of her knowledge. He must appreciate the value of silence and considered response before he is initiated and allowed to pass through the pillars towards greater knowledge.

ASSOCIATIONS AND SECONDARY IMAGES

Most of the High Priestess's associations are with the Moon, the Roman Luna or Greek Selene. Veritas, as the Roman goddess of truth, has her place, as does Fides, goddess of honesty; Themis, the Greek goddess of justice, and Ma'at, the

Egyptian goddess of order and balance.

CRESCENT MOON The crescent Moon at her feet symbolizes the High Priestess's understanding of her own sense of being. She is young, without blemish and not yet mature. Her task is to initiate, to create new beginnings.

CROSS The equal-armed cross on her breast is what is sometimes known as a solar cross. It signifies the balance between any two polarities: good and evil, light and dark, male and female.

FLOWING ROBES The High Priestess's robes, used initially to hide what she knows, change to become almost water-like, highlighting the inherent symbolism of emotion and power.

HEADDRESS The High Priestess's headdress is a powerful symbol that demonstrates her allegiance and status as Lady of the Moon. It signifies the waxing, waning and full Moon, and today is accepted as a symbol, or sigil, to signify three potential aspects of woman: maid, mother and crone.

PILLARS The pillars have several significances. One is the doorway to greater knowledge, the second is the duality inherent in humanity. They are also a depiction of the horn and ivory pillars at the entrance to Solomon's temple, signifying the polarities from which creation is said to have begun. The B and J stand for Boaz (the Feminine Principle) and Joachim (the Masculine Principle), also thought to mean maker and redeemer.

SCROLL The scroll signifies ancient knowledge. Inscribed with the word Tora, it denotes her own spiritual truth, which she chooses to keep concealed.

VEIL Decorated with palms and pomegranates (symbolizing knowledge, learning, wisdom, victory and fruitfulness), the veil suspended between the two pillars conceals the mystery of those joys to come.

KEY FEATURES

ELEMENT Water.

PLANET The Moon.

NUMEROLOGY This card is designated 2, signifying duality and fluctuation between two polarities.

DEITIES Luna/Selene, Veritas, Fides, Themis, Ma'at.

KEY WORDS Consciousness. Change. Fluctuation.

RELATED CONCEPTS Sophia as the principal of wisdom. She is the root essence of consciousness; the regulation of the flow, direction and energy of vibration.

THE EMPRESS

O mother earth, kindly set me down upon a
well-founded place! . . . O thou wise one,
do thou place me into happiness and prosperity.

Atharva Veda

THE IMAGE

The Empress card is given the number 3, representing stability. The image is of a woman seated facing us, in some packs with wings coming from behind her back. She wears a crown and holds in one hand a sceptre topped by a globe, signifying the power she has to create a perfect world or a state of near perfection. Elsewhere in the card is the symbol, or sigil, for Venus, representing femininity. Her flowing robes highlight her maturity. In some illustrations she carries a shield depicting an eagle – a symbol of royalty and the spirit. Surrounding her is a field of corn ready to be harvested. To one side is a waterfall in the midst of a grove of trees.

THE SIGNIFICANCE

The Empress is, by nature, the feminine ruler, life-giver, counsellor, open to all, practical and decisive. In the Tarot, she represents woman, mother and domestic happiness – the female life-giving force. When under pressure she can show disloyalty and a tendency towards stagnation, sterility and unproductiveness. She warns also of the potential to put others before herself, often to her own detriment. Our traveller on this part of the journey meets the full force of feminine energy. He must come to terms with the inexorable creativity that the Empress, as the fruitful mother of thousands, generates. Just as a youth must understand his mother in order to mature fully and use his creativity, so a girl must appreciate the full potential of her own femininity as a maid, mother and wise woman. As part of the adventure, our traveller learns to appreciate the cyclical aspect of Mother Nature and that there will always be a harvest – a consequence of his actions – whether good or bad.

ASSOCIATIONS AND SECONDARY IMAGES

The main association with the Empress is with the fecund corn goddesses such as Demeter and Hera, symbolized by the field of corn. In addition, she has an understanding

of the qualities of Venus, the goddess of love and beauty. She also has connections with Isis, who is said to have brought about the resurrection of her husband Osiris; through sheer tenacity she found all the various parts of him that had been scattered to the four winds. Venus is her controlling planet.

CROWN The Empress's crown or diadem symbolizes her royal status. It is frequently shown as having 12 stars, designating her the queen of heaven, and is also said by some to represent the 12 tribes of Israel, while others say the stars signify the 12 houses of the zodiac.

CUSHION OR SEAT Her cushion or seat, in raising her above her mundane surroundings, symbolizes her control of the more destructive aspects of love. She has much to teach others, but does so in a caring, nurturing way.

SCEPTRE AND ORB The prominent image of the sceptre in her hand also denotes her royal status and her right to rule, particularly within the feminine realm. The orb symbolizes

the world, and by extension the cosmos, which cannot exist without her presence as mediator. It is her perception which brings about a balance.

TREES AND FOREST The trees and forest visible in the card are a threshold symbol. The Empress must move forward with courage into new experiences. It is likely that in order to move forward properly, those who come to an understanding of her must undergo some form of initiation or undertake a special task.

WATER AND WATERFALL The water and waterfall depict the flow of energy and power necessary for creativity. Out of that energy arises emotion, and

the ability to use the power of that emotion successfully.

KEY FEATURES

ELEMENT Earth.

PLANET Venus.

NUMEROLOGY Designated 3, this signifies enterprise and a period of waiting for results or an outcome.

DEITIES Demeter, Hera, Venus, Isis.

KEY WORDS Unity. Pleasure. Fertility. Builder of form.

RELATED CONCEPTS The universal mother. The power of love. Pure emotion. The union of the masculine and feminine principles to bring about manifestation. The divine feminine power.

THE EMPEROR

*Knowing others is intelligence; knowing yourself is true wisdom.
Mastering others is strength; mastering yourself is true power.*

Tao Te Ching

THE IMAGE

The Emperor card is designated number 4. The number is indicated more than once in this card: there are four rams' heads, and the Emperor sits four-square on his throne of stone. Esoterically, four is the number of pragmatism and manifestation – both qualities inherent in the Emperor. An older man, he is power made manifest and wears his rich robes of office comfortably. He knows that under those robes he is protected by the armour of experience, and dares anyone to thwart his command. In one hand he holds the orb representing the physical world and in the other the ankh, an ancient symbol of eternal life. On his head is a crown, drawing attention to his intellect and designating him as royal and untouchable. His throne is decorated with rams' heads and behind that lies a mountainous country, in some packs edged by a river.

THE SIGNIFICANCE

The Emperor is the counterpoint to the gentler feminine energy of the Empress. Often taken to represent a father, father-figure or mentor, the Emperor – while always prepared to accept responsibility – can also find it a burden. Under these circumstances he can become mean-spirited and controlling. Then he becomes rigid and unbending and somewhat child-like in his responses. Given the opportunity to show his maturity, however, he develops much more into the kindly father role.

Our traveller finds in him all the enthusiasm, energy and assertiveness with which he began his own journey, but this time directed to more self-centred ends. Strong-willed and to a degree autocratic, the Emperor teaches him the art of leadership and how to create a firm basis for the empire that he, the traveller, will create in the future. He must be pragmatic and down-to-earth, but also aware of the legacy he will leave behind.

ASSOCIATIONS AND SECONDARY IMAGES

The main associations for the

Emperor are those of authority and leadership. As the good general, he is both Roman Mars the warrior, and Jupiter the father-figure. As the demiurge, the creator or controller, of Platonic thought, he fashions already created material and gives it form. Thus he makes things real.

Mars is also the Emperor's controlling planet.

ANKH This cross appears frequently in the Major Arcana in one form or another. Here it is both protective and a sign of eternal life stretching as far back as Egyptian times and the beginning of magic.

ARMOUR The armour the Emperor wears protects him from external attack but also gives him the confidence to carry out his task. It is his sense of rightness that carries him forward and allows him to meet challenges head-on and with courage.

CROWN The Emperor's crown symbolizes the intellectual ability to enable him to be an effective ruler. It is not flamboyant, but again points to his innate authority and right to rule.

ORB This 'sphere of completeness'

highlights the Emperor's ability to form his own domain and rule over it. It also indicates his grasp on the material world and everything that signifies.

RAMS' HEADS There are two potential significances in this crucial image. The Emperor has been assigned to the sign of Aries, signifying his ability as a leader. The second significance is slightly more subtle, indicative of a potential state of transition from leadership in the more mundane world to the spiritual aspects of a follower, a disciple or member of a flock.

RICH ROBES In colour versions of the cards, it is apparent that the robes are in two shades of red. The first is that of the purely physical arena; the second,

a rich burgundy, indicates that the Emperor is in touch with the spiritual realms and works wisely and well.

KEY FEATURES

ELEMENT Fire.

PLANET Mars.

ASTROLOGICAL SIGN Aries.

NUMEROLOGY This card is designated 4, which signifies he is solid, tangible and stable, uniting physical and spiritual principles in one whole.

DEITIES Zeus, Jupiter.

KEY WORDS Energy. Authority. Creative force.

RELATED CONCEPTS Ambition and achievement. Initiation of energy. Divine masculine power.

THE HIEROPHANT

Intuition is the clear conception of the whole at once.

Johann Kaspar Lavater (1741–1801)

THE IMAGE

Given the number 5, this card begins to interpret and explain the esoteric Mysteries. The Hierophant is pictured seated between two pillars, which are topped by carved lotus flowers symbolizing those Mysteries. In one hand he holds the triple cross, the insignia of his leadership of the Church on Earth, while his other hand is raised in blessing. His direct gaze is towards us, the implication being that he imparts knowledge of the hidden realms. He wears a triple crown, again demonstrating his supremacy over all worldly things. Often known as the Pope, he is served by two tonsured priests or monks in rich vestments. He has at his feet two crossed keys, and round his shoulders is a narrow band called a *pallium* – both are symbols of his power.

THE SIGNIFICANCE

Whereas the Emperor signified power within the ordinary world, the Hierophant signifies power within the spiritual one. He imparts spiritual knowledge and is the link with the Divine. Through him we have access to the Mysteries, yet at the same time

his power as leader of a hierarchy of belief must be acknowledged. This illustration contains much symbolism that does need to be understood before we become sufficiently perceptive to contemplate the next part of the Journey of Life.

In meeting the Hierophant, our traveller begins to learn more of the spiritual realms. The Hierophant's task is to reveal the unknown, but in such a way that it is understandable within the constraints and strictures of the everyday world. As the Fool begins to appreciate the enormity of the task ahead, the Hierophant is there with wise counsel. If, however, the Hierophant's counsel is ignored, then any progress is halted. The traveller must now learn to be the bridge between the sacred and the secular, and to listen to the subtler vibrations of life.

ASSOCIATIONS AND SECONDARY IMAGES

The main association for the Hierophant is spiritual authority, whether that be papal authority, Christ, or our connection with source through the shamanic

journey. Worship of the Persian god Mithras pre-dated Christianity and contained many similar principles. The feminine energy is represented by the acknowledgement of Venus. Through the Hierophant, we come to some understanding of the interplay between spirituality and the mundane and the channelling of spiritual energy for the benefit of all.

CROSSED KEYS The crossed keys are the keys to heaven and earth and symbolize the right of entry into both domains. As always, this right of entry must be earned by proving ourselves worthy, then awaiting acknowledgement of our right to be initiated.

CROWN Now no longer used to indicate spiritual authority, the three-tiered ornate crown here signifies teacher, lawmaker and judge or – more spiritually – priest, prophet and king.

EARFLAPS OR LAPPETS In the Rider Waite Tarot pack, the earflaps symbolize the Hierophant's ability to hear and to listen carefully to what is occurring in both his domains. This is a quality which any initiate into the mystery of existence must develop.

MONKS AND VESTMENTS The two monks illustrate the duality that must be appreciated as our experiences encompass polarity. Their vestments, richly decorated with roses and lilies in many packs, reiterate the theme of pure thought.

NECKTIE OR PALLIUM This again reinforces the idea of spiritual ascendancy and suggests, in the small crosses that often appear on it, the stages of initiation that must be gone through before esotericism is fully understood.

PAPAL CROSS OR FERULA This is a three-barred cross, with the crossbars in diminishing order of length towards the top. In downward order, they signify the celestial, human and material worlds. An archbishop's cross has two bars and the third bar is apparently added to indicate a rank even higher than that of archbishop.

KEY FEATURES

ELEMENT Earth.

ASTROLOGICAL SIGN Taurus.

NUMEROLOGY This card is designated 5, indicating supremacy and the necessity for change.

DEITIES Mithras, Venus.

KEY WORDS Illumination. Teaching. Spiritual instruction.

RELATED CONCEPTS Teacher and guardian of the Mysteries. Connecting the macrocosm to the microcosm.

THE LOVERS

The most important thing in life is to learn how to give out love, and to let it come in.

Morrie Schwartz (1916–1995)

THE IMAGE

This card is assigned the number 6, esoterically signifying the entry of spirit into matter. Two naked innocent figures, one male and one female, stand to the right and the left at the bottom of the card. The Tree of Knowledge is behind the woman, with the serpent twining round it. Behind the man is the Tree of Life with flaming branches, perhaps again representing the 12 signs of the zodiac or the 12 tribes of Israel. The woman is aware of the angel above, who appears to be blessing them. Power and passion are represented by the flames of the angelic headdress and the full Sun behind. In the background is a mountain signifying, as it often does, difficulties that must be overcome.

THE SIGNIFICANCE

This illustration represents the coming together of masculine and feminine energy, initially in a very innocent way, then later to create a passionate force. In some ways this can be both a unifying and a disruptive strength.

The Fool now begins to understand how the duality of logical male energy and feminine intuitive power can be brought together to access a much more potent force. Through that unification something new and different can be created; yet at the same time our traveller must remain aware of the more sensitive aspects of his personality and perhaps tap into a higher purpose. In mundane terms, if he is to succeed, he will need the help of a willing partner and associate, someone who understands him and can be a mirror for his aspirations. It is at this point in his journey that he can become more orientated towards someone other than himself. He now has the right to make choices as to how he will live his life.

ASSOCIATIONS AND SECONDARY IMAGES

There are several associations that can be made with this card. Usually its ruling sign is thought to be Gemini, along with Mercury,

the Roman god of communication. Interestingly, because of the Sun pictured at its height and the flame-haired angelic figure, there may also be an association with the archangels. This figure is often said to represent Michael, 'who is like unto God', but could also well be Uriel, 'the light or fire of God'.

FIGURES OF NAKED MAN AND WOMAN These symbolize innocence and joy as experienced in Paradise, before the Fall. The man looks towards the woman, who steadfastly returns his gaze, signifying that it is through her intuitive power that the man will come to understand divinity.

MOUNTAIN AND CLOUD Both of these images are in their own way indicative of the force of love, but are also representative of decisions to be made. The lovers may go the way of earthly desire and lust (the mountain) or may choose the higher option and explore together the more spiritual path (the cloud). Either way, they will brave together the difficulties that beset them.

TREE WITH FLAMES A representation of the Tree of Life, this suggests that the masculine figure is aware of the power of his inner passion. He must learn to direct this effectively as love in both its lower and higher aspects – carnal desire and union with the Divine.

TREE WITH SERPENT This signifies the temptation to try to understand all that is hidden within the Tree of Knowledge. Such knowledge, though, comes at a heavy price that – while bringing light on a subject – requires an understanding of the difference between right and wrong.

KEY FEATURES

ELEMENT Air.

PLANET Mercury.

ASTROLOGICAL SIGN Gemini.

NUMEROLOGY This card is designated 6 and signifies the building of communication and trust within a relationship of any sort.

DEITIES Mercury, Hermes.

KEY WORDS Liberation. Inspiration. Divine love. Fusion. Bonding.

RELATED CONCEPTS Freedom through unity. The integration of the spiritual with the basic urges. Union with the higher self.

THE CHARIOT

Dream as if you'll live forever, live as if you'll die today.

James Dean (1931–1955)

THE IMAGE

Assigned the number 7, which is considered by many to be the number of perfection and the control of magical forces, this card shows a young charioteer ready to drive forward two sphinxes. One is black and one white, indicating any two polarities – active/passive, good/evil, negative/positive and so on. In his hand the young man holds a sceptre or rod, while on his shoulder pads are representations of truth and revelation. These are the divinatory tools that are said to sort believers and non-believers from one another – another aspect of choice. His headdress is the eight-pointed star, signifying the gifts of knowledge still to come. Waxing and waning Moons form part of his shoulder pads, symbolizing increase and decrease.

There are also several other representations of duality in this card, such as the symbol on the front of the chariot representing the *lingam* within the *yoni*, a Hindu symbol suggesting the sexual act and the source of all life.

THE SIGNIFICANCE

The Chariot symbolizes choice and decision, followed by a triumphant ride. Any charioteer must first control the drives and aspirations inherent in his two horses and in his own competitive nature and must have the former work as a team towards a common goal. This charioteer's armour is his protection, his skill is not in question, yet he must call on his own experience to formulate the best way to move forward.

When our traveller meets the chariot on his journey, he understands perhaps for the first time the true meaning of responsibility. If he is to triumph over difficulty, he must make the right choices and be able to justify his decisions. These are not now just about him, but are about the welfare of others, and the effects his decisions will have on them. The symbolism is of the will, but of the will tamed.

ASSOCIATIONS AND SECONDARY IMAGES

The main association of the chariot is of the Greek Sun god, Apollo, driving across the sky in triumph. It is also the concept behind the story of Buddha in his cart drawn

by the white ox – that of being true to ourselves. The Chariot card is ruled by Cancer and the Moon. The inherent qualities of nurturing and caring are uppermost, having overcome the potential for destructiveness.

ARMOUR AND BELT The armour is shown as being quite ornate, designating the charioteer as being able to defend himself. The belt, however, although it is a sword belt, does not seem to carry a sword, so it would seem that it is more a mark of attainment than a practical object.

CASTLE/CITADEL There are two representations shown, to the right and left of the main image, one with much softer lines than the other. They again signify the duality of the masculine/feminine balance between the rational and intuitive.

HEADDRESS Looking almost like a miner's lamp, the light on the charioteer's forehead suggests intellectual enlightenment and clarity of purpose. It references the Star, a later card, which stands for his own personal truth and awareness.

SPHINXES These crucial images represent ancient wisdom and basic drives. The charioteer must use strength of purpose to bring these all under control. One of the sphinxes seems more wayward than the other, and both seem to be looking directly at us, willing us to understand.

SQUARES The chariot itself is almost cubic in construction. This, and the square on the charioteer's breastplate, suggest a grasp of the magical art of materialization and grounding within the physical world.

WINGED ORB This winged Wheel of the Spirit symbolizes the raising of the act of consensual sex – symbolized by the *yoni/lingam* – out of the mundane world. It gives it the status of the sacred marriage or union with the Divine.

KEY FEATURES

ELEMENT Air.

PLANET The Moon.

ASTROLOGICAL SIGN Cancer.

NUMEROLOGY Designated as 7, the art of manifestation and magical meaning.

DEITIES Apollo, Buddha.

KEY WORDS Will. Success. Eminence. Glory.

RELATED CONCEPTS Ambition, decisiveness. Control of subtle energies. Movement through all planes of existence. Manifestation of power in the mundane.

STRENGTH

Inward calm cannot be maintained unless physical strength is constantly and intelligently replenished.

Buddha

THE IMAGE

In the Rider Waite pack, the card number 8 is called Strength or Fortitude. A woman dressed in white subdues a lion by gentle restraint. She is linked to the lion by a garland of flowers tied around the waist, while above her chaplet of flowers is the sign of infinity (the number 8 turned on its side). In some packs, the lion's tongue protrudes from its mouth and its tail is between its hind legs as a sign of submission rather than triumph. Interestingly, that tail does not always end in a conventional tuft, but sometimes in more of a three-sectioned leaf-like shape. In the background is a mountainous landscape with a green fertile field in front.

THE SIGNIFICANCE

In many ways this is one of the sparsest illustrations in the pack, yet is easy to interpret as the quality most needed at this stage of the journey. The qualities of strength and fortitude are epitomized in the lion. The quiet force and inner strength available to the female figure are also made apparent.

By using her courage and skill she ensures that the animal does not become aggressive, but remains loyal to her and her principles.

As he progresses on his journey, our Fool gradually learns of the characteristics needed to continue on his way. The first of these is Strength and Fortitude. This is not aggressive in any form, but is the courage of conviction, gently applied to his own sense of power and majesty. He can thus overcome his own raw strength by willpower and achieve all that he needs to reach his goal. He has made his choices through the Chariot and must now stand by his decisions. Only then can he be initiated into the deeper Mysteries.

ASSOCIATIONS AND SECONDARY IMAGES

The lion appears in many cultures associated primarily with courage but also with majesty and power. The astrological sign of Leo is assigned to this card, giving an association with Ra, the Egyptian Sun god. The concept of the prudent use of energy

also gives an association with Brighid, the fiery goddess of the Celts and patron of blacksmiths and the art of poetry.

GARLAND OF FLOWERS A garland is a binding force. Made of flowers it denotes joy and happiness, so in this illustration it signifies the bonds of loyalty we form in life. It is also in this case a representation of the cords that bind the initiate in Masonic symbolism, which is often apparent in the Rider Waite pack.

HEADDRESS OF FLOWERS This is a rather subtle allusion to the idea of gentleness being converted into a strong will through intellectual means. Additionally, one alchemical tenet is that a lesser or base element, by the application of a higher energy, can be converted into gold. In this image, gentleness is converted into strength of purpose and an ability to use that strength wisely.

LEMNISCATE OR SIGN OF INFINITY This links with the idea of 'what goes around comes around' and the inevitability of karma (reaping the consequences of our actions). It also represents endless

being and eternity and a complete lack of boundaries and restrictions.

LION'S TAIL Tucked out of harm's way, in this image the tail signifies willing submission to a more potent force. In acknowledgement, perhaps, of the esoteric meaning of the threefold aspects of humanity – body, mind and spirit – it also signifies control of passion.

MOUNTAIN Sometimes perceived as a phallic image, the mountain here retains the idea of a potential problem that can be overcome. This is in the sense of overcoming logic and rationality – both masculine qualities – by gentleness and sensitivity in an effort to succeed.

KEY FEATURES

ELEMENT Fire.
PLANET The Sun.
ASTROLOGICAL SIGN Leo.
NUMEROLOGY This card is assigned the number 8, representing the union of the physical and spiritual realms and an understanding of the concept of spiritual energy.
DEITIES Ra, Brighid.
KEY WORDS Control. Courage. Resolve. Fortitude.
RELATED CONCEPTS Harnessed and controlled passion and loyalty. Power through gentleness. Energy through activity.

THE HERMIT

THE IMAGE

Given the number 9, in this case reinforcing the idea of spiritual knowledge entering the physical realms, the Hermit is pictured as an elderly man holding a light aloft in his right hand. This is a star enclosed in a lantern, yet he is looking downwards. In some representations the lamp is hidden in the Hermit's dark cloak, suggesting that he keeps his knowledge hidden. The figure is bearded and hooded and holds a staff or rod in his left hand. He stands in snow on top of a cold mountain and it would appear to be night.

THE SIGNIFICANCE

This card represents isolation, and with it a degree of negativity. The Hermit has climbed to the peak of knowledge, but may have become cut off from the rest of humanity in the process. His light now must be used to illuminate not only his own path but also that of others. He remains hooded, symbolizing that at this point he takes no real pleasure in the task, and still remains separated from others within his own understanding of himself. He knows that he is protected by his esoteric knowledge and trusts that he can safely go out into the world, yet hesitates to do so.

When our traveller meets the Hermit, he is faced with a different aspect of himself. He needs time to sit and contemplate those things he now knows and put them into some kind of usable framework. He must take time to clarify his beliefs, to decide what is of value to him and what can be discarded as superfluous. He understands that he is now truly on the path to enlightenment, that he will learn much by being self-sufficient, at the same time knowing that his universe will provide for him.

ASSOCIATIONS AND SECONDARY IMAGES

Most systems of belief contain the image of a pilgrimage, special task or period of introspection undertaken in order to gain greater knowledge or clarification. In some senses the Hermit card depicts a microcosm of the Hero's Journey, setting out

without knowing what will happen either to him or to others. The rod he uses to support himself has associations with the Rod of Aaron, a powerful tool to be used wisely and well.

The hermit can only journey forward trusting himself and his god. In Saturn and Chiron, he must acknowledge the healer within. The associated zodiac sign is Virgo, acknowledging the need to serve humanity in some way.

HOODED CLOAK This aspect of the Hermit suggests that he chooses to hide his intellect and knowledge from those he does not consider worthy. He will pass by unrecognized unless others seek his knowledge and wish to share with him.

LANTERN As a recognized carrier of light, in this instance the lantern signifies that the Hermit bears his own light with him. That is, it is his own understanding of power that illuminates his path ahead.

LIGHT In this card the important image of the light source is in the form of a six-pointed star. The image

is first seen in the headdress of the Charioteer. Its two triangles represent truth – matter aspiring to spirit conjoined with spirit descending into matter. The Hermit must now use his own truth in the mundane world with good effect before he can make use of it in a more esoteric and spiritual sense.

ROD Using his previous experiences as support, the Hermit's rod represents the potential for growth. He has reached the pinnacle of endeavour and although his environment is rendered somewhat inhospitable by the snow, he can afford to rest for a while and contemplate the way forward.

KEY FEATURES

ELEMENT Earth.

PLANET Chiron.

ASTROLOGICAL SIGN Virgo.

NUMEROLOGY This card is assigned 9, often thought of as the descent of spirit into the mundane world. It signifies placid acceptance of that which must happen.

DEITIES Saturn.

KEY WORDS Divine intervention. Inspiration. Divine wisdom.

RELATED CONCEPTS The Wanderer or Traveller. Bearer of illumination. Divine direction.

THE WHEEL OF FORTUNE

Nobody can go back and start a new beginning, but anyone can start today and make a new ending.

Dr Maria Robinson

THE IMAGE

This card has been given the number 10; in ancient symbology it represents the number of completion. This is a culmination of a previous way of being, the turning of the wheel – the Wheel of Fortune. Beyond this point on the journey, rather than there being an element of chance in what happens, there is recognition of opportunity and a willing acceptance of the good things that life brings. At the four corners of the illustration are the four Living Creatures, representing variously according to belief, the four fixed signs of the zodiac, the four Evangelists or the four classes of creature on Earth. Clouds billow around; a sphinx crouches on top of the wheel, while falling away from the wheel are carnal desire in the form of the serpent and temptation in the form of the devil. The wheel itself has the letters 'T O R A' inscribed on it, symbolizing truth, so this card might well also be called the Wheel of Truth or Justice.

THE SIGNIFICANCE

Just as a turning wheel changes things, so this wheel represents the change in fortune that occurs when we place the knowledge we have accrued in its proper context. The bad things fall away, matters begin to work out for us and we welcome good fortune.

Now the traveller, by his persistence, has earned the right – through self-contemplation – to good fortune and joy. His fears and doubts have been dealt with, he is not open to the temptations of the everyday world and he is ready to move forward into a new phase of understanding. At the same time, though ready to move on, he will not set out on his journey until he understands how best to make use of this good fortune.

ASSOCIATIONS AND SECONDARY IMAGES

The main associations for this image are the Tibetan Wheel of Life or *samsara* (the physical world), the zodiac, and the Rosicrucian *Rota Mundi* (the art

of interpretation). Some regard the symbolism as deriving from the Ancient Egyptians, associating the ascending and descending figures with Horus and Set and thus the eternal balancing of good and evil. Another association and ruler of the card is Jupiter, the planet of good fortune, through which we may lose in order to gain.

FOUR LIVING CREATURES With one at each corner of the image, the four Living Creatures mentioned by Ezekiel in the Bible are said to form a tetramorph, a composite representation of an idea. Here they represent knowledge of the human state through the symbolism of astrology. The fixed signs symbolize stability and, reading clockwise from top right, are Scorpio, Taurus, Leo and Aquarius. They also represent the idea of investigating more thoroughly what is already under way.

LUCIFER OR THE DEVIL This figure represents the ego, the more conscious part of ourselves. Without proper management we cannot make available

our own intrinsic honesty or inner truth – demonstrated by the wheel – within the everyday world.

SERPENT OR SNAKE This image symbolizes the lower, originally more monstrous, side of our urges. These can be transmuted from raw, untamed energy into a passionate creative force once they are brought under control.

SPHINX This image gives the tetramorph form within the physical, with the head of a pharaoh and the body of a lion, albeit apparently showing a female breast. Its tail appears to be that of a bull. The sword the sphinx carries in some images suggests the ability to cut through to essential meaning – a quality belonging to

Scorpio. The sphinx is a set point of reference and stability, the use of intuition to understand humanity's fate.

KEY FEATURES

ELEMENT Water.

PLANET Jupiter.

ASTROLOGICAL SIGN The complete zodiac.

NUMEROLOGY This card is assigned the number 10, suggesting that at this point a change occurs, spiralling our energy into a higher dimension.

DEITIES Horus, Set and Jupiter.

KEY WORDS Karma. Fortune. Time. Destiny.

RELATED CONCEPTS The Tibetan Wheel of Life. The Rosicrucian *Rota Mundi*. Rebirth and reincarnation.

JUSTICE

The mark of a good action is that it appears inevitable in retrospect.

Robert Louis Stephenson (1850–1894)

THE IMAGE

This card is given the number 11 – a master number – suggesting an intuitive grasp of spiritual matters. It portrays a somewhat androgynous royal figure seated between two undecorated pillars. He/she wears a crown and holds a set of scales – a conventional symbol for justice – in the left hand and a sword in the right. The robes in which the figure is dressed are rather voluminous, covered by a cloak falling from the shoulders, similar to those worn by priests. This designates a connection with spiritual matters and with moral rightness rather than judgement. Often the Justice card seems to be posing a question that requires a balanced opinion for an answer.

THE SIGNIFICANCE

In many ways, this card reflects the imagery of the High Priestess and the Hierophant, in that all three suggest the idea of a portal through which we must pass. In this instance, matters must be weighed carefully and cant and hypocrisy (weasel words) cut through to reveal the truth. Only then can the threshold be crossed and entry into the inner sanctum take place, where initiation into deeper mysteries can be accepted.

After his period of introspection, our traveller must weigh up his past actions. Equally, he must recognize that if he is to continue on his journey he should be true not only to his principles, but also be aware of the moral judgements of others. He needs to develop a degree of impartiality and achieve dispassion. Guided not just by his own needs, but also by his understanding of others, this may require some adjustment on his part. It may also mean that there are trials and temptations to be gone through before he reaches his goal.

ASSOCIATIONS AND SECONDARY IMAGES

The main associations for this card are the Greek goddess of divine law and order, Themis, and Ma'at, the Egyptian goddess of divine wisdom. A secondary association is with the Egyptian god Anubis, who weighed

the hearts of the departed and decided if they were worthy to continue into the afterlife. Both Themis and Ma'at were oracular goddesses and therefore pronounced – as dreams often do – on the correct conduct. The astrological sign awarded to Justice is Libra, whose sign is the scales. This suggests a state of equilibrium, not just in the mundane world, but an essential balance between spiritual and material matters.

CROWN This crown is what is known as castellated, thereby representing civic government; in other words, a caring for the welfare of the many rather than the few.

PLAIN PILLARS These are a threshold symbol, which cannot be passed through until certain matters have been taken into consideration. The passageway is shrouded by drapes, suggesting that beyond is unknown, perhaps scary, territory. As in the Hero's Journey, the seated figure offers tools that will help in our passage.

ROBES AND CLOAK The implication here – particularly because of the richness of the robes and the appearance of the stole – is that this figure is present by divine decree; his right to rule is not in dispute. He is also able to dispense wise words.

SCALES In life as in death our actions and principles must be weighed in the balance. Due consideration should be given not just to our actions but also the consequences of those actions. In moving into a new phase of existence we become more responsible for our own conduct.

SWORD This is a symbol of power but also of courage and rightness. Upright, this image signifies the warrior or fighter in each of us. When the point is downwards it suggests dedication to a cause.

KEY FEATURES

ELEMENT Air.

ASTROLOGICAL SIGN Libra.

NUMEROLOGY This card is assigned the number 11; again, a master number, indicating an instinctive knowledge of spiritual matters. When utilized properly the number 11 is a natural teacher and only under difficulty reverts to 2.

DEITIES Themis, Ma'at, Anubis.

KEY WORDS Equilibrium. Balance. Trust. Inner truth.

RELATED CONCEPTS Essential adjustment. Harmony and moral principle. Right action and right thought. Self mastery.

THE HANGED MAN

If you realize that all things change,
there is nothing you will try to hang on to.

Lao Tzu (c. 6th century BC)

THE IMAGE

Given the number 12 (3 × 4), this card signifies the completion of a spiritual cycle, perhaps the beginning of a new way of life. A young man hangs upside down on a living tree, tied by one ankle. His other leg is bent at the knee, forming the figure 4 or a fylfot cross – originally an ancient cosmic or religious symbol thought to bring good luck. His arms are tied behind him and a halo, or nimbus, shines around his head. In some representations of the card, coins fall from his pockets. He does not seem distressed by his predicament but is mostly contemplative.

THE SIGNIFICANCE

This illustration is probably one of the most important ones in the Tarot. It signifies sacrifice, not in the sense of giving up what the young man possesses of value, but in the sense of making it sacred. This is an act of dedication to a higher authority within himself and also the awareness that he

creates his own good fortune. This is life in suspension, which actually carries no pain. What it does is allow the young man to contemplate the world from a new perspective and therefore draw different conclusions, perhaps those he has never before considered.

When our traveller comes upon this figure, he is put in the position of having to question himself. He can no longer expect the answers he needs to be given to him when he demands them, but must wait until they arise from his own perceptions and understanding. He must have clarity of vision. Just as meeting the Hermit resulted in introspection, so meeting the Hanged Man results in an exploration of how he wishes to live life differently, becoming more aware of the spiritual values around him.

ASSOCIATIONS AND SECONDARY IMAGES

Perhaps the most widely known representation of the Hanged Man is

Odin. He was the Norse God who hung from Yggdrasil, the world ash tree, for nine days in order to obtain enlightenment. This image therefore does not represent martyrdom – dying for one's faith – but, rather, living for it. Such an act represents meditation carried to its highest degree in order to comprehend divine Mysteries.

This card is ruled by Neptune, also known as Poseidon in Greek mythology. The idea of penetration is present in the trident of Neptune, representing a threefold approach. By harnessing illusion and intuition we receive inspiration, allowing clarity and self-denial to inform our actions in the name of a greater cause.

HALO A halo is a representation of innate spirituality when perception is refined – as is the Hanged Man's. In dreams, it can also become visible when conscious restriction is removed.

LIVING TREE The *axis mundi*, the cosmic tree, is a universally recognized symbol. It is a point of connection for the Hanged Man between the upper and lower realms of existence and between the sacred and secular. He becomes the centre of his own universe.

TAU CROSS The Tau cross, in the shape of a T, represents life and resurrection. One of the most ancient symbols there is, it has always symbolized attainment and is also known as St Anthony's cross. St Anthony was the founder of monasticism.

LIMBS In creating a definite shape with the limbs, attention is drawn to the symbol of the Indian fylfot cross or swastika. Used in the correct way, unencumbered by the weight of 20th-century European history, it symbolizes the Wheel of Life and picks up an earlier symbolism of life continuing no matter what trials befall us.

KEY FEATURES

ELEMENT Water.

PLANET Neptune.

ASTROLOGICAL SIGN Capricorn.

NUMEROLOGY 12, which is a higher vibration of the number 3 – spiritual outcomes as opposed to practical.

DEITIES Odin, Neptune/Poseidon, Mother Earth.

KEY WORDS Sacrifice. Suspension. Trance state. Self-denial.

RELATED CONCEPTS Sacrifice of self. A period of withdrawal and suspended animation. Transcendence of the mundane. Cleansing of past misdeeds.

DEATH

As a well-spent day brings happy sleep, so a life well spent brings happy death.

Leonardo da Vinci (1452–1519)

THE IMAGE

This image has been numbered 13, a figure surrounded by superstition. Thought by many to be unlucky, it also signifies the ending of one cycle and the beginning of another. The image itself echoes this idea, consisting of an armoured skeleton riding a pale horse. The flag he carries is of the Mystic Rose, while under the horse's feet lies a supine king. A maiden and a young child show themselves to be fearful of the figure, while a prelate raises his hands in supplication. Overall shines a brilliant Sun. Sometimes a representation of the River Styx flows between two pillars in the background, along which the soul journeys to immortality or eternal life.

THE SIGNIFICANCE

Interestingly, this card is not as negative as it first seems. It represents a change of state and the realization that death does come to us all, whatever our status in life. The promise is, however, of a better life to come, provided we learn to understand that the ending of a previous state of affairs also heralds a new beginning. We may be fearful, but our path is clear. The suggestion of the River Styx is that we will need help to overcome the ill feeling that is almost inevitable.

When the Fool reaches this point in his journey, more than anything he has to face the idea of death. He has come a long way since he first stepped out, but realizes that he is not completely invincible, that there will come a time when death is inevitable. Before that, he must reach into his own depths and find the courage to continue. There is some bitterness and mourning for what might have been, but now he can let these go, knowing that to look back will only impede his journey.

ASSOCIATIONS AND SECONDARY IMAGES

Attributed to Pluto and Scorpio, this card follows an alchemical principle, the idea of transformation from base material to something meaningful. This image is quite

biblical in that it is Death sat on a pale horse (*Revelations 6:8*). This is one of the four Horsemen of the Apocalypse. These are night 'mares' indeed, but they do bring about change, transformation and purification. The Grim Reaper, as he is known, at first appears fearsome until it is realized that he actually brings about a change of state where one is free from physical difficulties and emotional shackles. Such a new beginning permits a fresh approach and often a transmutation of energy into something more usable.

FLAG AND ROSE The Mystic Rose on the black flag is said to symbolize unfolding consciousness, but is also a representation of the Virgin Mary and hence purity.

HORSE The horse has spiritual connotations in this card in that it represents the death of the old self and a new spiritual awareness. This particular one is said to have power over death by sword, famine, pestilence and wild animals.

MAID AND CHILD These two figures in the foreground reinforce the idea that death comes to everyone, no matter how we choose to meet it – whether that be with fear, denial, or the innocence of the untutored child or that of the more knowing maiden.

PLUMED HEADDRESS This represents the soul or life force and echoes the feather in the Fool's cap and that in the Sun's child's chaplet.

PRELATE The only upright figure, it is suggested that the prelate is praying for mercy by virtue of his beliefs, or that he awaits a 'good death' and an easy transition of awareness.

SQUARE TOWERS These towers denote the portal between concerns of the physical, mundane world and mystical knowledge.

SUPINE KING This figure underneath the horse suggests that death is a great leveller and takes no account of status.

KEY FEATURES

ELEMENT Water.

PLANET Pluto.

ASTROLOGICAL SIGN Scorpio.

NUMEROLOGY 13.

DEITIES Hades, Kali.

KEY WORDS Transformation. Transmutation. Change. Purification.

RELATED CONCEPTS Measured return. The Grim Reaper. All endings, often bringing about new beginnings. Constant cycle of death and rebirth. Radical change.

TEMPERANCE

Our attitude towards life determines life's attitude towards us.

John N. Mitchell (1913–1988)

THE IMAGE

This card is numbered 14 and in many ways represents the calm before the storm. A genderless angel with widespread wings stands on the edge of a pool, with one foot in the water and one on dry land. It holds two chalices in its hands, the left higher than the right. It is difficult to tell whether the liquid is flowing down or up. On one side of the illustration is a reed bed with yellow irises, and on the other an image often repeated in Tarot of the Sun coming up over the horizon, this time between two mountains. The angel's halo is very similar to the Sun and on the headband is another Sun symbol in the form of a circle with a dot in the middle. In many packs there is a path that leads from the pool towards the Sun.

THE SIGNIFICANCE

The card of Temperance suggests the principle of refinement once the balance between masculine drive and feminine intuition demonstrated in the image of the chalices is understood. This refinement compares to how iron is refined through fire into steel. Two opposites can be reconciled and the energy of them becomes more powerful as a result of that blending. Understanding emotion (the water) and yet being able to be properly grounded (the foot on earth) suggests the ability to make use of the full inherent power of the Sun.

Now our traveller is faced with something of a conundrum. He feels a rising sense of excitement within, yet also an equal sense of dread. The world around him is brighter and he knows he must continue his journey in order to maintain the flow. Before doing so, however, he must find moderation within, a dogged determination to use both the tools of his own passion and the practical lessons he has learned so far.

ASSOCIATIONS AND SECONDARY IMAGES

Temperance is associated with flow in the same way that the Egyptian god Hapy is associated with the flow of the life-giving Nile. Sarasvati (literally meaning 'knowledge of self'), the Hindu goddess of learning, brings about harmony and is also associated

with a holy river, the Sarasvati mentioned in the *Rig Veda*, the ancient collection of Sanskrit hymns. Iris, Greek goddess of the rainbow, is charged with bringing about correct communication and integrity.

This card is traditionally under the rulership of Sagittarius, though this is sometimes questioned. However, in the sense that the blending of opposites brings about clarity, it is appropriate. The successful amalgamation of instinct and intelligence in the centaur, this sign's magical creature, imparts vision.

CHALICES The chalices are symbolic of the source of inexhaustible sustenance, lifeblood and the Holy Grail. A chalice has associations with the boon or elixir obtained by the hero in the Hero's Journey.

HALO As with the Hanged Man, this halo signifies the spirituality and increased perceptivity that becomes available once we are no longer afraid of the transitions which must inevitably take place.

HEADDRESS The solar band, with the sigil for the Sun on the front, reinforces the idea of clarity of vision.

As we become more accustomed to seeing clearly, we have more understanding first of how to use this ability for ourselves and secondly how to use it in the service of others.

IRIS The iris plant is associated with new endeavours, hope and communication, and so suggests the confirmation of a new phase of existence; a welcome change from the more gloomy Death card.

PATH The path to the Sun sets out clearly the best way to achieve the goal we have set ourselves. As a dream or meditation image, it clarifies what must be done in order to achieve success.

KEY FEATURES

ELEMENT Fire.

PLANET Jupiter.

ASTROLOGICAL SIGN Sagittarius.

NUMEROLOGY This card is assigned the number 14 and therefore can be expressed as 1 + 4 equalling 5. This suggests necessary change. As 2 × 7 it is the combination of particularly subtle energies.

DEITIES Hapy, Iris, Sarasvati.

KEY WORDS Reconciliation. Arbitration. Combination. Fusion. Balance.

RELATED CONCEPTS The Holy Grail. Trial and temptation. Mediation. Water as source of life. The tempering of opposites.

THE DEVIL

We are each our own devil, and we make this world our hell.

Oscar Wilde (1854–1900)

THE IMAGE

This card has the number 15 – which can be interpreted numerologically in many ways. It is 10 + 5, symbolizing the fulfilment of logical, inevitable change; it can also be 9 + 6, thereby representing the linking of spirit and matter suggesting conscious awareness, and possibly ego. All these interpretations are clearly echoed in the image of the card.

An archetypal devil sits on top of a stone. He has bat wings and goat's horns – his lower half is also that of a goat. He is a representation of Baphomet or Lucifer, who was given the task of bringing enlightenment (conscious awareness) to humankind. This devil has a reversed pentagram touching the centre of his forehead. Attached by chains to the stone are male and female imps with animal tails; the female's tail is formed from a bunch of grapes, the male's is tipped by fire. This echoes the firebrand held in the devil's left hand. His other hand is raised in an apparent sign of blessing, although the intent is the opposite of this.

THE SIGNIFICANCE

This card is essentially about temptation. It is the temptation of allowing the ego to get the better of us and to believe that we are more powerful than we really are. Power used in the wrong way can be evil, and on the surface the devil appears to control the imps, yet without them he would be nothing.

Here, our weary traveller comes up against his own demons and need for power over others rather than the power he needs to succeed in his final goal. He is aware of his own raw energy; its use to control others is entirely seductive. If, however, he does not learn to handle his own desire for power and the changes that will bring, the knowledge he has acquired becomes debased.

ASSOCIATIONS AND SECONDARY IMAGES

The main associations are Lucifer and his alternative concept of Satan. The former was originally an angel sent by God to bring light into the world, who – forgetting his original

task – came to believe he was more important than the light itself and began to expect others to follow him. At that point he succumbed to the call of the ego and refused all attempts to return to heaven, being content to be both vilified and worshipped as Satan.

Baphomet, another association, is thought by some to be a pagan god and presents himself in the form of a horned god similar in appearance to Satan. In fact, he probably approximates more closely to the Greek nature god Pan – the god of fertility and lust. The card is ruled by Capricorn, the mythical sea goat who, through sheer determination, succeeds in bringing together passion and power.

HORNS AND BAT WINGS These are negative representations of night, evil and power generated largely through human fear of the dark. Horns generally are a symbol of the life force inherent in each of us; the imps also have small bud-like horns. The bat wings are a very ancient symbol of evil associated with spell-making and control of others.

IMPS The imps are representative of the lower urges. It is difficult to decide whether they are chaining the devil or vice versa. The male's tail represents passion. The female symbolizes, alternatively, fertility and joy.

PENTAGRAM The pentagram is a five-pointed star. When the tip points down rather than up, it signifies the physical world ruling over the spiritual, and has therefore become associated with the dark arts and with evil. Correct development of the third eye chakra in the centre of the forehead requires that it is used spiritually for the greater good.

KEY FEATURES

ELEMENT Earth.

PLANET Saturn.

ASTROLOGICAL SIGN Capricorn.

NUMEROLOGY Assigned the number 15, its 5 + 5 + 5 formation suggests radical adjustment on all levels – body, mind and spirit.

DEITIES Baphomet in his original form, Pan.

KEY WORDS Materiality. Temptation. Mirth. Ego.

RELATED CONCEPTS Occult science and dark magic. Sexual energy and reproduction. Illusion and distortion. Natural forces.

THE TOWER

Be as a tower firmly set; Shakes not its top for any blast that blows.

Dante Alighieri (1265–1321)

THE IMAGE

This card is allotted the number 16. In a similar way to the last card, this one can also be read numerologically. It is 8 + 8, which signifies a type of duality – the balance of spiritual and material – taken to its ultimate point. It is also 4 × 4, which symbolizes tangible material multiplied. It is this concept that gives us the image of a tower built on top of a hill or mountain. Exactly how many floors there are is unclear. The top of the tower is in the shape of a crown and is blown off by a bolt of lightning. This has caused fire in more than one area in the centre of the tower, since there are flames coming from two different levels as well as the top. Two figures are falling from the tower, both head first, and with fearful faces.

THE SIGNIFICANCE

The Tower card is often considered to be extremely difficult to interpret, but once it is thought of in terms of a revelation, its meaning becomes clearer. A divinely inspired insight strikes right to the heart of whatever structures and boundaries we have imposed upon ourselves. This results in a need either to reject old ideas and concepts completely or to sift through the rubble of what is left and rebuild our lives in a new way. This may bring fear but is ultimately cleansing.

This is a huge turning point for the Fool on his journey. He must completely reject all preconceived ideas about what life means, must face his own fears and doubts and 'clean up his act'. Whatever impels him to do this will indeed be cataclysmic, but ultimately puts him in a different space and frame of mind. He may well set off in a different direction to the one he first mapped out, but this time it will be the right one.

ASSOCIATIONS AND SECONDARY IMAGES

Among the Nigerian Yoruba people, the goddess Oya is perceived as the spirit of tornadoes and lightning, earthquakes and any kind of destruction. She also is the spirit of change and transition. Thor, the Scandinavian god of thunder,

is much associated with this image, and indeed the Norwegians refer to lightning as *Thorsvarme* (Thor's warmth). In middle Europe it used to be thought that lightning was a sign of God's grace.

Another association of the card is with the Tower of Babel – that huge construction which attempted to penetrate the mysteries of God. When, through God's intervention, communication broke down between the builders it resulted in total confusion and conflict. The planet Mars may be taken therefore to be an apt ruler of this card since it signifies both war and bravery.

CROWN The top of the tower, which has been blown off, is in the shape of a crown, symbolizing the fact that neither status and power nor intelligence can withstand the revelation that outmoded ideas must be rejected.

DARKNESS Darkness surrounds the Tower and its inhabitants. This is truly the dark night of the soul when all the false constructs are revealed as such by the inspirational lightning flash. It is the very brightness of the lightning flash of revelation that enables the darkness to be confronted.

FALLING FIGURES The faces of the figures depict the fear engendered by a cataclysmic event. Forcibly ejected from the safety of their own construction, they have no idea how to deal with what has happened. It will take a radical change of focus for them to overcome the problems created.

FLAMES AND FIRE These symbolize cleansing power. The realization that has caused such havoc also clears away obsolete ideas. Interestingly, flames and fire also suggest a newly revived passion for life.

KEY FEATURES

ELEMENT Fire.

PLANET Mars.

NUMEROLOGY This card is assigned the number 16. It can be reduced to 7, the manifestation of magic – but is easier to think of as structure destroyed.

DEITIES Oya, Thor.

KEY WORDS Sudden revelation. Blinding flash of inspiration. Restructuring. Strife.

RELATED CONCEPTS The Tower of Babel. Demolition of outmoded beliefs. Dramatic realizations. Remodelling and re-evaluation of outdated and obsolete ideas and concepts.

THE STAR

For my part I know nothing with any certainty, but the sight of the stars makes me dream.

Vincent van Gogh (1853–1890)

THE IMAGE

The Star card is given the number 17, which can be broken down numerologically in several different ways. Whichever way this is done, however, it ultimately reverts to 8 (1 + 7), signifying the union and flow between the spiritual and physical realms. This number gives rise to the main image of the large eight-pointed star surrounded by seven smaller, similar ones.

The original Rider Waite card shows a naked woman leaning forward with her left knee on the ground and her right foot on – rather than in – the pool of water in front of her. In our illustration, she is sitting more comfortably, aware of the need for stability. She pours water from one of the ewers she carries into the pool, while water pours from the other, apparently forming several distinct rivulets. Behind her is a tree on which sits a bird, possibly an ibis. In some packs there are growing plants that, if looked at closely, possibly resemble small signs of infinity each with a central flower. In the far distance are mountains.

THE SIGNIFICANCE

In this card the eight-pointed star represents the light that shines when we have succeeded in developing our abilities. We begin to understand the necessity for personal guidance and knowledge. The naked figure pouring water in two distinct ways suggests that we must learn how to maintain the flow between the spiritual and physical world.

By now the traveller, having come through the maelstrom of his previous adventures, desperately needs guidance. The star is the light that is no longer enclosed in the Hermit's lantern or under physical constraint. It is free to guide him on the correct path. He himself has learned how to manage his material world and, like the old-fashioned sailors, he must learn to navigate by his own personal star. His path is lit by seven other stars, but he has now made a firm connection to the larger, main one.

ASSOCIATIONS AND SECONDARY IMAGES

The eight-pointed star is known in Christianity as the star of redemption

or regeneration formed when the corners of an octahedron (eight-sided figure) are extended or stellated. In Hinduism, in a slightly different form – two squares, one rotated 45 degrees on top of the other – the star appears as the Ashtalakshmi, the eight forms or 'kinds of wealth' of Lakshmi. The embodiment of beauty, grace and charm, she is also the goddess of light and of prosperity. In Roman mythology Venus fulfils this function and in planetary lore Venus is the morning and evening star.

This card also has an association with the story of Eve in Paradise before the Fall; she is pure perception and here has control of the waters of life. This in turn links with the astrological ruler of the card, the Waterbearer, Aquarius.

NAKEDNESS As a representation of innocence and pure beauty, this figure is completely without guile, showing concentration only on the matter in hand. It suggests the idea that we need nothing and have nothing yet everything will be provided.

SEVEN STARS These are variously thought to be the seven major planets or the seven stages of spiritual development. Understanding these principles leads to a better utilization of the energy inherent in the major star.

TREE AND BIRD It is a very ancient idea that birds are representative of the soul and that the ibis is symbolic of perseverance and aspiration. The tree is the Tree of Life, suggesting knowledge of still-hidden ideas.

TWO EWERS These echo the two chalices in the Temperance card except that, rather than the energy flowing between them, some is flowing into the Earth and thus rendering it fertile while the remainder is replenishing the pool. This highlights the idea of regeneration and renewal.

KEY FEATURES

ELEMENT Air.

PLANET Uranus.

ASTROLOGICAL SIGN Aquarius.

NUMEROLOGY Number 17, which tends to echo the meaning of 8 at a higher vibration – the correct flow of power and energy between the realms.

DEITIES Lakshmi, Venus.

KEY WORDS Meditation. Hope. Pure consciousness.

RELATED CONCEPTS Contemplation. The inner voice. The upper astral plane. The river of life. The idea of bird as soul. Eve before the Fall.

THE MOON

Everyone is a Moon, and has a dark side which he never shows to anybody.

Mark Twain (1835–1910)

THE IMAGE

This card is assigned the number 18. Numerologically, 18 can be represented as 3×6 when it represents all the unconscious urges that manifest in our minds during sleep. However, it is also 2×9, which implies that we are capable of developing something close to perfection through understanding our own unconscious depths. This describes the Dream Oracle very succinctly.

The image itself is of a tranquil full Moon with a face that simply watches. Beneath this is water out of which crawls a crayfish or lobster. A path stretches ahead, passing a dog on the left and a wolf on the right, both of whom are baying at the Moon. The path then progresses between two square pillars and off into the mountains. In some packs, the Moon itself is surrounded by alternating short and long rays. In many packs, water droplets or tear shapes appear to be falling from the Moon.

THE SIGNIFICANCE

If the card is viewed from bottom to top it is easily interpreted and allows us to trace our traveller's progress. He must come to terms with the need for self-protection symbolized by the lobster or crayfish and trust that his own negativity and fear can be managed. Arising from the deep unconscious (the water) beneath which his real life purpose has been hidden, it is possible to move slowly on to the path which goes past the positivity of instinct (the dog) and the negativity of untamed instinctive understanding (the wolf). Our attention is drawn to the reflective light of the Moon, which enables the traveller to take a long hard look at the influences and cyclical nature of life. Then he must pass between the pillars, moving through into unknown territory and perhaps a new dawn.

ASSOCIATIONS AND SECONDARY IMAGES

There are many associations with the card. The most easily recognizable is the Greek goddess Selene, later supplanted by Artemis. Her Roman counterpart was Luna, later supplanted by Diana. Hecate, a much darker Moon goddess, was much

associated with change and the ebb and flow of life. The Egyptian god Khonsu protected night travellers and, as the god of light in the night, was in charge of male virility. Nanna, also known as Sin (and sometimes as Enzu), is a Sumerian Moon god.

Somewhat surprisingly, the ruler of the card is Pisces, with the planet Neptune. A negative aspect of this is the creation of illusion with the potential to get lost. A more positive rendering is the recognition that the reflective aspects of the Moon can bring about inspiration.

CRAYFISH/LOBSTER This crustacean represents suppressed ideas and urges. Being a creature of the deep, it emerges from the unconscious – symbolized by the water – and must orient itself within the upper world. At this stage it is protected by its shell, reminding us that rigidity and focus of purpose can be beneficial.

DOG AND WOLF The dog here has a similar significance as the one in the card of the Fool. He is a faithful companion, but is instinctively alerted to danger and warns of that which he does not understand. The wolf symbolizes the wilder untamed side of the personality that, particularly under the light of the Moon, can run out of control.

PILLARS Their squareness signifies an understanding of the life purpose hinted at as the crayfish emerges.

TEARS/DROPLETS The Moon is traditionally in charge of the emotions and these tears symbolize the release of unconscious influences and past difficulties. This release allows an influx of new energy, which can be used to make progress on the Journey of Life.

KEY FEATURES

ELEMENT Water.
PLANET Neptune.
ASTROLOGICAL SIGN Pisces.
NUMEROLOGY This card is assigned 18 and reinforces the idea of there being several aspects of the unconscious, which must be harnessed before we can achieve complete integration.
DEITIES Selene/Luna, Artemis/Diana, Hecate, Khonsu, Nanna/Sin/Enzu.
KEY WORDS Subconscious mind. Illusion. Evolution. Progression. Femininity.
RELATED CONCEPTS Suppressed ideas and desires. Personal demons and gremlins. The River Styx and the passage between two worlds. Night-time revelation.

THE SUN

Don't ask what the world needs. Ask what makes you come alive, and go do it. Because what the world needs is people who have come alive.

Howard Thurman (1900–1981)

THE IMAGE

In the Rider Waite pack, this card is given the number 19. It is a card of completion, of having reached a new dawn and in numerological terms a change of pace (1 + 9 = 10, which reverts to 1). A small naked child with arms outstretched sits on a white horse. He carries a banner and on his head is a chaplet with a jaunty feather, echoing the feather in the Fool's cap Behind him are sunflowers. A huge Sun surrounded by wavy and straight rays looks on. In some packs there are two children.

There are strong similarities at this stage between the Fool's Journey and the Hero's Journey. This card, more than any other, emphasizes the moment on the Hero's Journey where he emerges from the underworld to bring back the elixir of life.

THE SIGNIFICANCE

The naked child suggests a rebirth into a new innocent state. The white horse is a symbol for spiritual awareness, while the banner the child carries symbolizes the standard of conduct expected from him. Tradition decrees that he is coming out of a walled garden, indicating that past restrictions are no longer relevant and that the Sun can shine for him at last. As sunflowers welcome the Sun, the child holds his arms wide to welcome a new way of loving.

This, for the Fool as he journeys onwards, is a definite high point. He has overcome many obstacles, some of them self-inflicted, has learned to understand himself and those around him and now can reap the rewards of his endeavours. In the child he recognizes his own innocence; in the Sun he finally understands that the ebb and flow of circumstances around him are much under his control. Life is now literally what he makes it – he is master of his own destiny.

ASSOCIATIONS AND SECONDARY IMAGES

The Sun represents a higher power, and there tend to be more Sun gods than goddesses. Initially, Moon was

masculine and Sun feminine, so where there are solar goddesses they are particularly significant. Sunna, the Norse goddess, rode her chariot across the sky during the day; Amaterasu, the Japanese Sun goddess, went into hiding behind a boulder by night. In Egypt, there was more than one Sun god – Kephri for the rising Sun, Ra at noon and Atum at the setting Sun. Apollo and Helios were both Greek, Sol Invicta was Roman.

The card is under the rulership of the Sun and signifies regeneration and joy. The Sun almost inevitably is associated with fertility, prosperity and the cycle of the seasons. These associations are a crucial aspect of our understanding of the card. Life-giving energy becomes available and we can then flow with the seasons, working according to the rhythm of life.

SUN'S FACE The face here is essentially masculine and appears to be looking straight at us, almost challenging us. It suggests that, by using reason and faith, we too can approach life with integrity.

SUN'S RAYS The rays of the Sun are wavy and straight alternately. This signifies a more sophisticated grasp of the life-affirming, subtle energies and qualities of light rather than that reflected by the Moon.

SUNFLOWERS Sunflowers are symbolic of adoration. In following the sunlight, they demonstrate the idea that no one can grow spiritually without the basic instinct of following a higher power.

WALL OR FENCE These symbolize the barrier between the inner or higher self and the outer expression of spirituality. When this outer expression is one of innocence and joy there is freedom, love and laughter.

KEY FEATURES

ELEMENT Fire.
PLANET The Sun.
ASTROLOGICAL SIGN Leo.
NUMEROLOGY Assigned the number 19, by calculation it reduces to 10, a more subtle vibration than 1 and therefore a new phase of existence.
DEITIES Sunna, Amaterasu, Kephri, Ra, Atum, Apollo, Helios, Sol Invicta.
KEY WORDS Conscious mind. Joy. Increased perception.
RELATED CONCEPTS Existence of higher self. Awareness of higher realms of being. The intellectual mind and the power of knowledge. Life-giving energy.

JUDGEMENT

To the mind that is still, the whole universe surrenders

Lao Tzu (6th century BC)

THE IMAGE

This card is numbered 20 (2 × 10) and as such highlights duality, not just on one level of being but on two – sacred and secular or spiritual and physical. The number ten represents both an ending and a beginning – it is the point of transition from a completed cycle to a new one. Since 20 is 2 × 10, this particular transition is especially meaningful.

An angel is shown blowing a trumpet that carries a flag with a cross. Beneath him are naked figures arising from coffins. There are three main figures: man, woman and child, suggesting that nobody is free from this final call. Other figures in the background show the same awe and adoration as the main figures. Where it appears in some packs, the water in front of the coffins is somewhat choppy and in the background are some inhospitable mountains – a recurring theme in the cards.

THE SIGNIFICANCE

The angel here sounds the Last Judgement. Now it is time for a kind of resurrection; those who have been asleep must waken and give accounts of themselves. Our traveller, who by now is more aware of the consequences of his actions, will work to come to terms with the past, whether that is past hurts, misdeeds, mistakes or misunderstandings.

He will take his time to listen to his higher self, his inner oracle, and will learn to forgive and forget. He will be enabled to let go of everything that has gone before and will put into perspective all he has learned on his journey. Though he is no longer the carefree young man who set out on that journey, he is still able to take life as it comes. Strangely he realizes that none of what has happened is either negative or positive, it is as it is. He has learnt to be dispassionate.

ASSOCIATIONS AND SECONDARY IMAGES

The main association with this card is that of resurrection and rebirth. Almost all systems of belief incorporate the idea of the raising of the dead. The resurrection of Christ and the descent into the underworld by the Sumerian

goddess Inanna to resurrect her husband Tammuz, confronting Erishkegal her destructive sister, both have this theme. The Hero's Journey highlights coming back into the land of the living. What is becoming known as psychological transformation suggests coming to terms with what has gone before. They all bring about a new beginning and a new awareness.

Pluto is the ruler of this card, and while he is pictured as the god of the underworld, his energy is also transformative, opening up new avenues of exploration.

COFFINS The coffins signify that those who have been made aware are able to leave behind the trappings of the physical and material realm. Traditionally they have overcome death and can now play due deference to the greater powers.

FLAG WITH RED CROSS A flag normally makes a statement. Long before the red cross usually seen on this card became well known as a modern-day charity logo it was a statement of commitment for the Knights Templar to preserve the values of Christendom. In this card it symbolizes loyalty.

MOUNTAINS AND WATER The overall feeling of the card is frequently taken as somewhat desolate and is often interpreted negatively. However, this time the imagery is more to do with what is past and with the promise that what is to come will be better. Life can begin again with added vigour.

TRUMPET An especially pure vibration is often symbolized by a trumpet, particularly as in this case when it is a wake-up call. The fanfare trumpet depicted here is most often used as an angelic instrument.

KEY FEATURES

ELEMENT Fire, Spirit.

PLANET Pluto.

NUMEROLOGY Assigned the number 20, this highlights duality to a higher vibration than 2 and indicates the need for new ideas and concepts. Radical change on all levels.

DEITIES Hades, Demeter, Erishkegal, Inanna.

KEY WORDS Initiation. Consecration. Verdict. Baptism of fire.

RELATED CONCEPTS All forms of resurrection. Eternal life. Awareness of the Divine. Being in receipt of divine energy. Spirit descending into matter. Use of discrimination.

THE WORLD

THE IMAGE

This card, numbered 21, in some packs called the Universe, again contains hidden information from a numerological perspective. It is 3×7, 3 representing stability and 7 signifying the organization of energy. This suggests, by extrapolation, the correct organization of energy on all levels of existence – body, mind and spirit. When our energies are correctly aligned we can find our own place in the universe, and this is ably illustrated by the image in the card.

The central female figure is semi-naked, protected by a spiral drape of material. In each hand is a double-ended wand and source of light, while surrounding her is a laurel wreath in the shape of an O or, in some cards, an oval, when it becomes the *vesica piscis* – the gateway to intuitive power. Outside this are representations of the four elements first seen in the Wheel of Fortune.

THE SIGNIFICANCE

This is the card of completion. Our Fool reaches the end of his journey and, just as the Hero has on his journey, he returns to the ordinary world, having gained understanding, undergone various trials and tribulations and faced his own demons.

He has reached a point where he understands the gifts that he has to offer the rest of the world. He has access to the information he needs to be able to help others; he can use his intuitive abilities to guide him on his way, but perhaps more importantly he understands that he is protected from, and can handle, whatever the rest of his life may bring.

He still has his dreams to sustain and guide him, but now when they frighten him he can discover their meaning and can use the power they give him. When he has difficulty in understanding others he now has the tools to unravel the mystery.

ASSOCIATIONS AND SECONDARY IMAGES

The Zoroastrian god Ahura Mazda – which translates as 'wise lord' – has the most natural association with the card of the World. This also means that any figure of wisdom such as a

holy prophet or religious leader – one who gives a wider viewpoint than a mundane perspective – is also relevant. From a feminine perspective the goddess Gaia, also known as Mother Earth, was the primordial element from which all gods originated in Greek mythology.

There are also associations with the Jewish Shekinah, the feminine principle of God. The card is considered to be ruled by Saturn in the sense that this planet gives form and weight to concepts and ideas by making them tangible.

FOUR LIVING CREATURES Also known as the cherubim, the Living Creatures in each corner of the card represent the elements, worlds and forces, which in their lowest form are seen in the Minor Arcana. Now more defined than they were in the Wheel of Fortune, they represent a cherub, lion, bull and eagle. These signify the four elements and essentials of understanding necessary to maximize our potential.

LIGHT SOURCES/WANDS The light source first appearing in the hand of the Magician is repeated here and seen in both hands, indicating complete control of natural forces. Not only is the central figure in control of herself, she is also now in control of the forces which shaped her.

LAUREL WREATH Symbolizing achievement and success, the wreath also brings to mind the Cosmic Egg, the source of all creation, or the Void, the no-thing that has the potential to be everything.

SPIRAL DRAPE This symbolizes the movement of energy both upwards and downwards between the spiritual and physical realms. This movement is both protective and energizing.

KEY FEATURES

ELEMENT Earth.

PLANET Saturn.

NUMEROLOGY The card of the World is assigned the number 21, representing three 7s, an alignment of perfect manifestation, and thus means 'I am'.

DEITIES Ahura Mazda, Gaia.

KEY WORDS Exploration. Achievement. Completion. Conclusion.

RELATED CONCEPTS Creation. The innocence and wisdom of understanding. The beginning and the end of everything that exists. The keys to the universe. The Cosmic Egg.

THE MINOR ARCANA

Whereas the cards in the Major Arcana highlight the inner journey that we must all attempt – the Fool's Journey – those in the Minor Arcana show the more ordinary, day-to-day events and how these affect us.

Our dreams can be enhanced by an appreciation of the meanings of each of the 56 Minor Arcana cards. In fact, because they relate to everyday events, in many ways it could be said that the imagery in the Minor Arcana is more relevant to the ordinary dream state than that in the Major. It will depend on your own perspective as to which of the two you feel are the most important.

It is not until we understand the individual symbols and how they work together, however, that we can begin to see their full significance; then everything begins to fall into place. Once we have a clear idea of what they represent, we will begin to be able to use them to help in dream interpretation and as ideas to enhance creative dreaming.

We first came across the symbolism of the Minor Arcana in the Magician card, where his tools are laid out on the table in front of him. As we saw, these are a pentacle or coin, a cup or chalice, a wand or stave, and a sword; and some of these tools appear in other cards in the Major Arcana.

HISTORICAL SYMBOLS

One familiar feature of the Minor Arcana is their similarity to the playing card deck that we know today, and this is because they gave rise to modern playing cards. The court cards in modern decks – King, Queen, Jack – are also a legacy from the original Tarot decks, in which they were depictions of people, characteristics or aspects of our own personality.

In the Rider Waite pack developed at the beginning of the 20th century, the numbered cards (called pips in playing cards) were given illustrations that helped to clarify the idea behind the relevant combination of each number and suit. Thus in the two of Wands, for instance, the figure is seen to be using the wands or staves as support. The wands are shown as budding branches, depicting the potential for growth. The card suggests the presence of a powerful, experienced figure – perhaps a successful businessman or woman who will act as a guide or mentor, working with you towards greater career achievements.

Many later Tarot packs followed similar ideas, and were heavily dependent on esoteric and Masonic imagery for the illustrations for the Minor Arcana. There is a more recent movement towards less heavily symbolic illustrations and a more intuitive approach to interpretation, though from a dream-image perspective the Rider Waite is the most evocative.

THE FOUR SUITS

Each of the four suits in the Minor Arcana is given an overall meaning. Originally, they symbolized the areas of life most important to the majority of people, particularly in an agrarian society. Popular belief, through the ancient game of Tarocchi, had it that originally the suits of the Minor Arcana represented the different strata of society. Pentacles represented the tradesmen, Cups the clergy, Wands the peasants, and Swords the aristocracy.

Later, as more people became knowledgeable about esoteric matters, the traditional meaning re-emerged that the four suits correspond to the four elements which form the basic energies of creation. Thus Coins (later called Pentacles) are Earth, Cups are Water, Sceptres (later called Wands) are Air and Swords are Fire.

In the ordinary, mundane world, therefore, the four suits broadly have the following symbolism.

PENTACLES Money, stability and material matters.

CUPS Love, happiness, harmony, sensitivity, fertility and unity.

WANDS Work, creativity, reputation, fame, enterprise and efficiency.

SWORDS Ideas and communications, hostility, struggle, bitterness and malice.

THE COURT CARDS

If the suits represent the elements, the four court cards in each suit represent individual types of people, each with their own characteristics.

So we have now seen that there are 16 court cards in the Tarot pack, each suit having a king, a queen, a knight and a page. The various symbolic interpretations of the cards overlay each other, so it is important to appreciate the significance of all the elements in order to see how they can enlighten the interpretation of your dreams. Thus, each court member brings certain significances to the interpretation, which are combined with the symbolism of the relevant suit. When dealing with the court cards, the characters each have their own personalities, giving specific interpretations to each one.

KINGS The kings are mature males, authority figures who embody power and rulership, achievement and responsibility. They represent good government. When a king appears in a dream, he might well represent your own desires and ambitions.

QUEENS Queens are mother-figures and persons of authority with the inherent qualities of fertility and feminine wisdom. They also represent religions or systems of belief. When a queen turns up in a dream, she will represent your own inherent power or the supportive side of your nature.

KNIGHTS Knights are young men and women who have not yet developed true maturity. They also symbolize learned behaviour. When a dream of a knight, soldier or warrior also contains a Tarot tool it suggests that the qualities symbolized by that particular suit need to be brought to the fore.

PAGES Pages refer to young people of either sex who have not yet found their metier or way of being, so everything is in potential. There may also be a link with the arts and sciences. In dreams a page will signify the child within – a part of the personality that is as yet hidden, but has the potential for considerable development.

THE COURT CARDS IN PENTACLES

Pentacles represent the material things in life, so the significance of the court cards is overlaid with meaning relating to the areas of finance and stability.

KING The King is a practical, honest and generous man who will inevitably make a success of his life. He is good with finances, often entrusted with the management of other people's resources.

QUEEN The Queen is hard-working and practical, a good businesswoman. She can come up with real solutions to problems, though without others quite knowing how she has done so.

KNIGHT The Knight is a stable character, highly organized and well aware of his own values. Unlikely to enjoy the limelight, he has a cautious approach and often prefers to be alone rather than in company.

PAGE The Page is the dependable young person who has a need for a secure environment. No matter what gender, this figure represents a loyal and steady friend and companion, though he or she can show distress if pushed beyond his or her limits.

THE COURT CARDS IN CUPS

Relationships are the key here, as love and unity are the key words associated with Cups.

KING The King is a highly emotionally oriented man. He is someone you can trust and respect and who always puts people – especially his family – first. He believes that people are innately good.

QUEEN The Queen represents emotional nurturing. She is creative, an intuitive healer, much in tune with others. Not easy to get to know, she keeps her own counsel, and can also be judgemental.

KNIGHT The Knight is the archetypal knight in shining armour, a true romantic who is on a mission to find the Holy Grail of Perfection.

PAGE The Page is essentially a dreamer, sensitive to others, both to their pain and their needs. Highly imaginative, he can become depressed if misunderstood.

THE COURT CARDS IN WANDS

Work and creativity are the areas associated with Wands.

KING The King is a mature man of vision who enjoys life to the full and does his best to ensure that everyone around him does too. Happy to share his wisdom, he makes an excellent boss.

QUEEN The Queen is independent and authoritative, imaginative and intuitive – a wise woman. She is only too happy to help in any situation but can be somewhat overwhelming.

KNIGHT The Knight is a great communicator with a love of travel and risk. Meeting life head on, his energy requires a degree of restraint to be used properly.

PAGE The Page is somewhat child-like, wholly exuberant and expecting to be noticed. However, given a task to fulfil, he or she is reliable, assiduous and focused.

THE COURT CARDS IN SWORDS

Communication is relevant here, combined with the court-card symbolism, as is struggle and sometimes hostility.

KING The King is a very fair-minded individual who has the tendency to hold himself apart from others. Principled in the extreme, he has very high ideals and expects much from others.

QUEEN The Queen is loving and kind, though on first acquaintance, or until you gain her trust, she seems aloof and critical. She relies on facts and will share her information willingly if asked.

KNIGHT The Knight is an 'up and at 'em' character, sometimes creating conflict purely for the pleasure it gives him. He makes an able champion, if he feels those he loves have been wronged.

PAGE The Page is a clever and humorous, young-at-heart individual. He or she can be very aware of, and will champion, human rights, but has a tendency to speak before he or she has fully thought things through.

THE NUMBER CARDS

Additionally each numbered or 'pipped' card has a specific concept attached to it, both from general esoteric numerology and from the Tarot suit, which you can bring into play when you are using Tarot in dream interpretation.

In the dream section we highlight the general importance of numbers, shapes and patterns. In the Minor Arcana, the numbered cards tell their own story, and are illustrated in a way that also demonstrates some of the significance of number. As before, the combination of number and suit symbolism gives us the key to interpretation.

In dreams where we are particularly aware of there being a number of something – whether that be an article, idea or repetition – we can discover the implications by understanding the relevance of number.

This can help us interpret the symbolism of our dreams. In addition, contemplation of a card within the Minor Arcana, taking into account its numerical esoteric interpretation as well as its suit meaning, can act as a trigger for a series of dreams that can inform our actions in everyday life. We will examine this further in Dream Management.

THE SYMBOLISM OF NUMBER

There are widely accepted esoteric meanings associated with number *per se*.

ONE The seed or beginning of things, one represents unity and the creative principle within the individual.

TWO Two represents duality, receptivity and partnership. It is indicative of diversity or polarity. Compromise and the achieving of balance are inherent in this number.

THREE This number signifies new beginnings, birth, life and death. Any aspect where things become visible or manifest – have an outcome – belongs to three.

FOUR Four is solid, tangible and stable, uniting physical and spiritual principles in one coherent whole. The number four unites the four elements and gives form to matter.

FIVE Power, domination, victory and change are symbolized by five. There is sometimes a tension between construction and destruction, enforcing necessary change.

SIX Six signifies hesitation and difficulties in communication that can be smoothed over. Opposition is managed by the building of trust.

SEVEN Seven is the organization of universal energy into useable tools and tangibility. This is the holy or cosmic number, which initiates vast transformation.

EIGHT Eight signifies the union of the physical and spiritual realms and is therefore the number of transcendence. Inevitably there is fear attached to this process, but this can be overcome.

NINE The number of initiation, of endings and beginnings, nine sometimes signifies passivity, and suggests acceptance. It forecasts the return to unity.

TEN Finally, ten reassures us that there is always hope and positive change. Nothing is permanent – a continual process of regeneration takes place and there is promise of a new phase of existence, perhaps to a higher vibration.

THE NUMBER CARDS IN PENTACLES

Specifically Pentacles relate to the material aspects of our lives – money, stability and practical goals.

ACE Often representing dreams of material gain, this suggests prosperity gained through hard work.

TWO Harmonious change and the balance achieved through good management is indicated by two, as is a fruitful partnership.

THREE Three indicates management of financial resources and gain through commercial dealing.

FOUR Financial gain, often through a gift or successful negotiation, is symbolized by these Pentacles, usually associated with a down-to-earth approach.

FIVE Five suggests a loss of money or status, recoverable only after hard work. It can signify a lean period involving some confusion.

SIX Material success is suggested by six, often through teamwork or good leadership.

SEVEN There is unfulfilled success despite good management of resource, seven suggesting that something more is required.

EIGHT Eight highlights prudence, yet small gains, with slow but steady growth.

NINE Material gain, possibly through inheritance, can show a way forward.

TEN Wealth, prosperity and the successful completion of a project relate to ten.

THE NUMBER CARDS IN CUPS

These are the symbolic associations of the number cards in Cups, the suit that signifies the emotions and suggests love, happiness and harmony.

ACE Happiness and pleasure are indicated here, as well as fertility and creativity. The ace is often taken to represent the horn of plenty.

TWO Love and harmony, unity and mirth are all relevant to two, as is emotional integrity.

THREE Abundance and plenty are related to three. It indicates an overflow of good fortune, pleasure in personal success and in the success of others.

FOUR Partial success, which may be something of a mixed blessing, may lead to instant gratification, which can distract attention from the ultimate goal.

FIVE Five suggests loss of pleasure and potential disappointment although, while some good things may be lost, there is the potential for future happiness.

SIX Pleasure and the enjoyment of sharing and receiving are symbolized by six. There is a suggestion of a steady increase in good fortune, sometimes through caring about others.

SEVEN Seven represents success through the use of one's innate talents. The contemplation of options and opportunities is indicated, not least because some may be illusory.

EIGHT Effort and courage are required when eight is indicated. It suggests abandoning success and the rejection of that which is no longer necessary or relevant.

NINE Material happiness and the pleasure that generosity engenders relate to number nine. It indicates the realization and emotional contentment brought about by one's own efforts.

TEN Perfect success and, through this, true happiness symbolize ten, with quiet contentment and celebration at the outcome of projects.

THE NUMBER CARDS IN WANDS

Wands symbolize creativity and the world of work, the energy needed for growth and efficient functioning.

ACE Natural force, energy and strength need to be strategically applied.

TWO Power and status are gained through the use of authority. Success can be achieved through bold action and planned activity.

THREE Established strength and manifestation of success is indicated. It highlights self-assertion and the ability to be generous.

FOUR Indicating work perfected and properly grounded, this can represent property or a completed project bringing about security.

FIVE Conflict and argument are signified, along with rash behaviour and aggression, sometimes just for the sake of it.

SIX Six indicates victory and success through perseverance, and pleasure in overcoming obstacles.

SEVEN Courage, particularly in the face of opposition, and the use of intellectual abilities to the best advantage are symbolized here.

EIGHT Much associated with quick thinking, though sometimes applied too forcefully, this is related to opposition and quick-fire communication that can be easily misunderstood and is not always to be trusted.

NINE Strength and powerful energy are associated with nine, particularly energy specifically applied to achieve maximum results despite self-doubt and possible health issues.

TEN Struggles due to an excess of external pressure suggest growth is possible, but only if the individual's needs are satisfied.

THE NUMBER CARDS IN SWORDS

Swords suggest a degree of hostility and struggle – ideas and communication need to be made more tangible despite difficulties.

ACE The power available for both good and evil and the fight for justice and a return to basics are indicated here.

TWO Peace is restored after conflict, perhaps involving lack of tact and understanding. Selfish acts can lead to tension in relationships.

THREE Sorrow and heartache are associated with this card, often for more than one reason. It can indicate thoughtless actions causing problems that appear difficult to resolve.

FOUR There can be rest from strife, although further action may be required. Struggle is no longer necessary.

FIVE Defeat, though more through resignation than force, can show that lessons are learned the hard way. Victory does not necessarily bring pleasure.

SIX Goals can be reached through hard work. Success is achieved, though often at some emotional cost.

SEVEN Uneven efforts yield only partial success and may mean that opportunities may have to be reconsidered. Others may prove to be untrustworthy.

EIGHT Force and energy are curtailed by external conditions. Wisdom and clarity of vision may not have been used correctly.

NINE Waking from a bad dream, distress causes some difficulty but life must go on.

TEN Circumstances forecast doom and disaster. Time will heal the difficulty provided integrity is maintained.

The Fool's Journey, which we now accept as psychological development and spiritual growth, was initially a simple visual way of helping people to understand themselves. The Tarot in its entirety therefore offers a kind of encyclopedia of human experience forming a structure – a warp and weft – on which we can hang our dreams. First, however, we must learn to move towards our own inner wisdom through the art of dream management.

DREAM MANAGEMENT:
HARNESSING CHANGES IN OUR CONSCIOUSNESS

Dreaming has long been accepted as an altered state of awareness that occurs spontaneously during sleep. There are, however, a number of other changes in consciousness that can, with practice, be harnessed in order to awaken our inner oracle.

In this section we shall explore daydreaming, creative visualization, meditation and dream manipulation as tools in understanding and maximizing our own inner potential.

DAYDREAMING

This state does not require us to be asleep. It uses that part of our brain that needs to idle – to take time out from our ordinary everyday lives. It is a way of exploring possibilities and opportunities without putting ourselves at risk. It has been discovered that what was assumed to be lack of activity is, in effect, an altered state of consciousness that can be used as a precursor to creative visualization.

CREATIVE VISUALIZATION

This is the next stage in bringing some regulation to a wayward mind in order to manifest our desires. Rather than the random daydreaming and 'Wouldn't it be lovely if . . .' scenario, creative visualization sets out to have us paint an inner picture of what it will be like actually to have what we desire, manifest what we need and be what we want to be.

MEDITATION

The stilling of our mind that we achieve in meditation gives us more conscious access to hidden images and ideas. These, once allowed to surface, offer us deeper penetration into the universal knowledge and energy that lies beneath the surface of the mind – the collective unconscious. This knowledge is hidden from us until such times as, through continuous calm contemplation – the true definition of meditation – we can give our mind a point of focus but at the same time allow it to roam free.

DREAM MANIPULATION

An extension of both creative visualization and meditation, dream manipulation can be used both to understand dreams and perhaps even to bring a dream to a better conclusion. By consciously putting ourselves back into the dream and visualizing a different outcome or a different scenario, we can often change our reaction and response to the dream.

Once we have clarified what information our inner oracle has been attempting to give us, we can enhance our understanding by using all four of the above methods, ultimately incorporating Tarot into the process. We can then consciously monitor our own behaviour. As we become more proficient at understanding our dreams, we can learn to adjust our later dreams through a form of witnessing – observing without judgement. By becoming more aware of a greater spiritual reality, we are capable of moving beyond a self-centred approach to life.

DAYDREAMING

Daydreaming, or reverie as it is sometimes known, has been defined as the thoughts of an individual that are apparently unrelated to what is going on around them.

When we daydream, the brain takes time out to idle – to stand down from a mechanical task, perhaps, or to consider options of action in the immediate future. Similar to dreaming during sleep, the average person's brain idles about every 90 minutes. This seems to be in response to biological fluctuations in temperature, coupled with hormonal activity.

CHILDREN DAYDREAMING

Most children begin to daydream at approximately the age of three, though it apparently is not until later, around the age of ten, that they begin to actually internalize this spontaneous mind-roaming. These early daydreams seem to set the pattern for later ones; children with happy, positive dreams of success and achievement ('Wouldn't it be lovely if . . .') tend to continue to have similar types of daydream into adulthood. They are then able to use this facility for problem-solving and creativity. However, those children who have experienced frightening images are more likely to be negative thinkers in adulthood, though with a modicum of training this can be remedied by using a positivity technique (see information panel).

POSITIVE BENEFITS

While it is true that daydreaming can be entirely whimsical, distracting and great fun, it is also true that it can have a degree of negative feedback in some cases. Daydreamers can come to prefer the slightly bizarre elements of the process; lonely people can get so caught up in daydreams that they isolate themselves from social contact. Obsessive thinking, for instance, can interfere with day-to-day activity. It has also been said that a wandering mind is an unhappy one, though perhaps in this case daydreaming may be a self-comforting mechanism.

Having said that, somewhat more focused reverie can open up many possibilities and have a very positive effect on our thinking. It has been found that it can:

- Induce relaxation by removing concentration from a stressful task or circumstance.
- Boost productivity by clearing the mind of intrusive and distracting thoughts.
- Relieve boredom by allowing the mind to remove itself from the task in hand.
- Boost creativity and achieve goals by imagining success.
- Maintain relationships by creating ideal scenarios.
- Manage conflicts by allowing the mind to consider alternative solutions.
- Cement personal beliefs and values by learning to categorize what is relevant.
  This makes daydreaming a powerful tool in our self-development armoury.

FOCUSED DAYDREAMING

It has quite rightly been said that we do not consciously use much more than 10 per cent of our brains. What *is* fascinating is what goes on in the other 90 per cent, and whether we can utilize it. Daydreaming is one way of using a little more of that hidden content, and focused daydreaming – applying a light rein to a wayward mind – utilizes it even more. Gently schooling the mind to decide on our own personal philosophy (see information panel), or using creative pursuits such as keeping a journal, painting, writing poetry and making craftwork, also paves the way for the next, even more focused process – that of creative visualization.

CREATIVE VISUALIZATION

Creative visualization is a very positive, self-affirming method of transforming our lives that moves us on from daydreaming.

As a preliminary to creative visualization, it is often necessary to experiment with our daydreaming and fantasizing and to decide what is comfortable for us. For someone of a particularly pragmatic turn of mind, it may even be necessary to relearn how to daydream!

When we daydream we tend to start off from the statement 'Wouldn't it be lovely if . . . .' Then as we get older, unless we have learned to focus more fully and be constructive, we will cancel this out by following up with 'But it will never happen.' We all have different ways of preventing ourselves from achieving what we want.

The use of spoken affirmations (see information panel) is one way of getting rid of our 'blocks to progress' and of influencing our lives so that things happen the way we want them to. For those who are perhaps not terribly eloquent, or who find that such a technique does not work for them, it may be better to use visualization rather than speech as a tool.

REINFORCING OUR DESIRES

Constructive daydreaming, creative visualization, and indeed using our dreams creatively, all work by affecting our unconscious self. They all let us give ourselves permission to be creative (have ideas) and often actually to create. The more we consciously reinforce our own desires, the more they are likely to happen. Thus it is vital to remember that part of this process is visualizing what we feel *can* be sustained when it *does* become real.

Unlike daydreaming – when anything is possible – if we use visualization, we should recognize that we must strive to achieve as much perfection as we can when we start. Here we immediately come up against a problem. What one person may consider perfect, another may not. As an example, one individual may decide that a focused visualization with complete detail is their idea of perfection, while

another may agree that detail is important but feel that the visualization itself should be comprehensive. A third person may feel that perfection is the actual manifestation (occurrence) of their visualization. Each person thus has their individual concept and learns to understand their own process of manifestation.

As time goes on, you will become more proficient at visualization, and will instinctively feel when it is time for you to move on to the next stage.

STAGES OF VISUALIZATION

Broadly, the stages of creative visualization are:

- Set the scene in as much detail as you can.
- Visualize yourself and others participating in your scenario.
- Refine the detail, rejecting those things that are obviously not feasible or are over the top, and accept and add additional detail where possible.
- See and feel yourself participating in your visualization (this is slightly different to the second stage in that your participation should feel more real. In other words, it should be possible).
- Test your doubts and fears. These may range from 'Have I the right to expect this?' to 'Someone will stop me . . .', taking in a huge range of similar such statements in between – even down to 'Do I really want this?'
- Accept that whatever you are visualizing can happen for you in the present. You are giving yourself an acceptable present.
- Take responsibility for allowing your visualization to happen. You have, and can have, a sustainable future.

AFFIRMATION

Do remember that these affirmations are only general starting points and that yours must be made specifically personal. Some to help you get started might be:

- I see myself as a successful person.
- My relationships support and sustain me.
- My emotions truly reflect the way I feel.
- My work is creatively satisfying.
- I allow my innate wisdom to help me make choices.
- I am able to create for myself an acceptable 'here and now'.
- I am able to create a future for myself that can be easily sustained.

Take some time every day to repeat the statement you choose, out loud if possible. Preferably repeat it in blocks of three to a total of at least nine times. There is good reason for this number in that, vibrationally, it confronts your own negativity, which will not allow itself to be challenged more three times.

It is no use visualizing what you want only once, then simply expecting it to happen. Begin by practising for a short time every day, preferably just before you settle down to sleep. This fixes your visualization in the subconscious and your dreaming self is called into play to assist in the manifestation of your requirements (see information panel).

Many people like to feel that they are co-operating with their own universe in which anything is possible. Others may feel more comfortable believing that they are drawing their requirements towards them – operating the law of attraction as it is now known. Each person will have their own particular idea.

While daydreaming can allow us to progress to creative visualization, exercising the art of creative visualization acts as a precursor to using our dreams more effectively. Finally, we can enhance our ability even further by using meditation.

MANIFESTATION

This technique is deliberately designed to be used over a period of ten days – ten being the number of change.

Visualize your wishes in as full a form as possible, including every little detail, however ridiculous, silly or unattainable you suspect them to be. Apply the first four points of creative visualization. Do this for a few minutes for three consecutive nights before you settle down to sleep.

For the next two nights, leave the visualization strictly alone. You need do nothing, though during this time you may find that you have to deal consciously with your fears and doubts. This allows you to highlight negative belief.

The next night, bring the picture to mind. Some of the details will have changed, some disappeared and some become sharper. This is known as the clarification stage, moving from what is possible to what is probable. This highlights what is unnecessary and allows you to concentrate more fully on what you instinctively feel is feasible.

For the next five nights, visualize the amended picture and apply the final two stages, acceptance and responsibility, while you do so.

Let the whole matter rest and await developments.

MEDITATION

Meditation gives us conscious access to images and ideas. This, in turn, allows us deeper penetration into the hidden knowledge that lies beneath the surface of the mind.

This knowledge tends to be occluded until such times as we give our mind a point of focus but at the same time allow it to roam free. This roaming occurs in daydreaming, is more focused in creative visualization and becomes even more so in meditation.

While dreaming, unless we have trained ourselves to dream creatively, this roaming happens spontaneously. When we learn to meditate, our inner oracle is initially more selective in choosing appropriate images out of the vast library of the collective unconscious. Meditation and dreaming share many of the images in this collective unconscious – therefore there is a similarity in the interpretation of those inner pictures. When the final stage of meditation is reached, a sense of tranquillity is attained where imagery becomes unnecessary.

As a discipline, meditation helps us to become more conscious of changes in awareness, both in the everyday and within the dream state. In a sense it allows us to be more present – within the here and now. It also has the effect of opening our minds to dreaming as a spiritual learning tool.

It is now known that both meditation and shamanism access the theta waves of the brain. These have a slower rhythm than both the beta and alpha waves of the waking state. The shamanic practitioner, for instance, brings about a change of consciousness in themselves, usually through such practices as auto suggestion. This, in turn, gives access to an enhanced inner reality of rich imagery and power.

Using the three Cs – Concentration, Contemplation and Control (see information panel overleaf) allows us all to be highly creative and often to be aware of what is needed for the greater good. Once you feel you have achieved this degree of control, you might like to try shifting your focus of attention to your heart and your heartbeat. Again using the three Cs, slow (control) your heartbeat. Given time, you may well be surprised by the sense of peace that prevails.

THE MANDALA

After you have learnt how to meditate, your dreams can take on a deeper clarity. For instance, the mandala, when perceived in dreams, can become a gauge for your spiritual progression. A sacred shape, the mandala is powerful enough to be found in one form or another in most systems of belief, though most often in Eastern religions.

Usually it is a circle enclosing a square with a symbol in the centre representing the whole of life. It is mostly used as an aid to meditation. The principle is that one travels from the outer circle (which stands for the whole of existence) through the creation of matter – the square – to what represents the centre of existence. Finally, one moves back out to take one's place in material existence again.

Often consciously depicted as an eight-pointed star, which we have already encountered in the Star card in the Tarot, the mandala represents both human aspirations and burdens. It frequently appears in dreams in this form, and can then become a personal symbol of the journey from chaos to order. It has also been found that, in a healing process, this symbol will occur over and over again. It is seen often as ornate pictures or patterns.

Having meditated using a mandala you might like to try concentrating on and contemplating a point in the centre of your forehead, just above your eyebrows. Without any expectation of a result, remain focused and, in due course, you should eventually become aware of a sense of spaciousness – what is now known as the Void. Sometimes there will initially be what appear to be swirling coloured or white clouds on the periphery of your vision, but this will soon settle down to what we have elsewhere called a sense of 'no-thingness'. As perceiver you are the only object within that space. The vastness can be both intriguing and frightening. With the heightened awareness comes the knowledge that our higher self – the part that knows what is right for us – is our own best oracle.

To understand our own journey from chaos to order, we must appreciate that this void is an aspect of the unknown that can be variously frightening or entirely tranquil. From the chaos of the untutored dream-state, via daydreaming, creative visualization and meditation, we can work towards understanding and utilizing our own Dream Oracle. To do this consistently and create order in our lives, however, we must learn to use the tool of dream manipulation.

POOL MEDITATION

There is a meditation or guided imagery technique which can enhance our ability to dream.

- First, picture yourself walking in a field.
- Feel, if you can, the grass beneath your feet and the wind on your face.
- Walk towards a slight dip in the ground which is to your left, traditionally the more intuitive side.
- At the bottom of this dip there is a pool which is surrounded by trees.
- Sit quietly by the pool, simply thinking about your life, perhaps recognizing some of the influences which have shaped the way you think and feel.
- When you are ready, stand up and walk into the pool very slowly.
- Feel the water rising slowly up your body

until you are immersed completely. (This is thought by some to represent a return to the womb-like state of awareness before birth.)

- At that point, let go of all the tensions of the everyday world and concentrate on the peace which is within, becoming aware of your own heartbeat and the rhythm of life.

- Slowly emerge from the pool and sit quietly beside it.
- When you are ready, walk back to the point in the field where you started and let the image fade.

By practising this regularly, particularly immediately prior to going to sleep, you will gradually find that dream images take on a deeper meaning.

CONCENTRATION, CONTEMPLATION AND CONTROL

There is a very easy way to think of meditation and that is by using the three Cs: Concentration, Contemplation and Control. These three concepts are used in each step of learning.

CONCENTRATION Concentrate first on your breathing and wait until it becomes slow and even. Contemplate your breathing as it flows in and out, just being aware of the process. Control your breathing until you have achieved a good rhythm (breathing in for a count of four and out for four works well; four in, hold for four and six out is even better).

CONTEMPLATION Choose an idea or concept to consider. Without any outcome in mind, concentrate on the idea and contemplate objectively what comes to mind. If your mind wanders, bring it gently back to the matter in hand, controlling and focusing your thoughts.

CONTROL Now, applying what you have learned, initially visualize a point in the solar plexus and concentrate on that point. Contemplate any thoughts or emotions that arise. Control your breathing, and as you breathe out just simply let them go.

DREAM MANIPULATION

Dream manipulation is a technique that can be used to enhance our understanding of our own dreams and further our understanding of the links between dreams and Tarot.

Sometimes in dreams there is an intensity of emotion that can be extremely frightening. We may be incapable of feeling such an emotion in everyday life, but for some reason can allow ourselves to be terrified in nightmares and bad dreams. With greater proficiency at dream manipulation, we can often change the outcome of a bad dream into a good one. Originally known by the acronym RISC, this technique was developed in the second half of the 20th century in America as a therapeutic tool to deal with bad dreams (see information panel). More positively, it can be used to manipulate less bothersome dreams. Once we have studied our dream carefully to our own satisfaction, we are able to take it forward and work with possible helpful conclusions. For instance, we might dream of driving a lorry that is out of control and about to crash into a brick wall. We wake up just before we hit the wall.

After careful consideration we decide that this mirrors a work-related issue over which we have no control. Considering more deeply, we first recognize that in the act of waking up we have become aware of the problem and have escaped from a bad dream. We can then consciously manipulate the ending of the dream to indicate a suitable way of dealing with the issue, at the same time remaining objective because it is the images with which we are dealing and not the situation itself.

Using the techniques of visualization, we can imagine ourselves jumping from the lorry before it crashes, thereby risking personal injury. Alternatively we might decide to crash into the wall and envisage ourselves being catapulted over the obstacle. We might drive round it or, if we trust our own judgement, decide it is an obstacle that, after careful consideration, has no validity and is therefore not a threat. At that point, we might decide that much the most

Because it takes approximately six weeks to make changes on a psychological level, you do need to be patient while learning these new techniques. Often, you will notice changes in attitude fairly quickly, but a change in behaviour does not become habitual until six to eight weeks have passed.

The four steps known as RISC are:

• **R**ecognize a bad or disturbing dream while it is occurring.
• **I**dentify the bad feeling.
• **S**top the dream.
• **C**hange negative into positive.

Initially it may be necessary to wake up in order to undertake any of these steps, but gradually, with greater proficiency, you will find you can do this while remaining asleep.

sensible action is to apply the brakes and take back control of the vehicle. We then apply that solution in waking life and slow down whatever was the impending headlong rush towards disaster.

Occasionally it is you, the dreamer, who is most surprised by the changes which then occur. You may become more able to deal with issues that have previously proved difficult, or find that inner conflict is more easily and efficiently handled. Rerunning the dream in your own mind when awake will usually show which adjustment is the best outcome for you.

USING TAROT SYMBOLISM

An extension of this method is to choose a Tarot illustration to clarify the issues. We might, in this case, choose the Emperor that – as we have seen – signifies control over the practical aspects of life. After carefully studying its meaning and secondary images, and perhaps meditating on it, you may

intuitively know how to resolve your problem. If the resolution does not become apparent, ask for the dream you want the next evening, using the CARDS method explained in the Dreams and Dreaming section (see page 81). With practice, you will be able to stimulate your dreaming mind into giving you the answers you need to help with difficult situations in waking life.

PATIENCE

Do remember that the dreaming self can be somewhat wayward, so initially the answer may not come to you on the night you request it. You may only receive part of an answer, or nothing at all for several nights, and then a series of dreams that tell you what you need to know. It is always a highly individual process and there is no given pattern. With time, you will recognize your own individual pattern, but be prepared to be patient with yourself.

When we combine Tarot, creative visualization, meditation and dream manipulation we have all the tools necessary to delve deeply into interpreting our own Dream Oracle. It speaks clearly and unequivocally to us in a way that no other oracle can. Let us then move on to understand the whole process of effective dreaming.

DREAMS AND DREAMING

The overall purpose of this section is to draw several strands of dream interpretation into a manageable whole and to make the information easily accessible. This means that you can choose to explore the world of dreams to the level at which you are comfortable. As with the other parts of the book, additional information is shown in information panels for ease of understanding. Also included are several dream interpretations to help the dreamer understand and interpret their own dreams.

In this section we have followed similar ways of categorizing the images as with the Tarot. We have:

Described the images.

Highlighted the broad significance of those images.

Widened perception by interpreting some of the actions associated with the image; this may be the object itself or an action by the dreamer. As an example, interpreting 'deep water' or 'going down into the water' requires the dreamer to have an understanding of both the overall symbolism of water, as well as the particular significance of whatever action is being undertaken.

Using as a basis the well-known quantitative analysis scheme of classification inaugurated by Calvin Hall and Robert van de Castle in the 1960s, we have chosen to divide the explanations and interpretations into comprehensive segments. Broadly the contents are:

The participation of the dreamer—the Hero's Journey and the Fool's Journey.

Settings and scenery – places and environments, buildings and structures, nature, ecology and plants, obstructions and obstacles, water, weather and time.

Characters and participants – people, family, animals, birds, insects, and mythological, magical and spiritual characters.

Interactions, qualities and principles – behaviour, actions and activity, occupations, belief systems, the body, and clothes and appearance.

Emotions, reactions and responses – positive interactions and celebrations, negative actions and interactions, relationships and intimacy.

Integral objects – furniture, food and drink, symbolic imagery.

Transitional elements – methods of transport and types of journey.

Endings and conclusions – waking up, deliberately waking up, logical endings.

Once all such aspects have been considered, we may then apply our techniques of dream management, incorporating asking for the dream we want using the CARDS method (see information panel). The Dream Oracle thus performs its function, allowing the dreamer full access to his or her own inner library of explanations.

CARDS METHOD

For this technique, you simply need to remember to use the word 'CARDS' as a memory jogger. The steps are:
• **C**larify the issue.
• **A**sk the question.
• **R**epeat it.
• **D**ream and document it.
• **S**tudy the dream.
C The first step means that you spend some time clarifying exactly what the issue really is. There is no need to try to resolve the situation at that point.

A You then ask a question with as much relevance as possible. Ask the questions 'Who? What? Where? When? Why?' and sort out in your own mind exactly what the relevant question is.
R Repeat the question at least three times and possibly nine. That way you are fixing it in the subconscious and opening up to the possibility that your Dream Oracle can give you the answer.
D Dream command means informing your inner self that you will have a

dream that will help. Document your dream briefly as soon as you can, noting down the main theme and the main and secondary images.
S Study the dream in more detail when you have time. Consider the imagery within the dream carefully; it will probably be fairly clear cut and straightforward. Look for details, clues and potential hidden meanings. Lastly, see if any of the images can be related to the Tarot.

THE DREAMER, THE HERO AND THE FOOL

Remember today, for it is the beginning of always. Today marks the start of a brave new future filled with all your dreams can hold. Think truly to the future and make those dreams come true.

Walter Winchell (1897–1972)

While dreams are totally spontaneous, they nonetheless have an inherent structure. To make the most of the effort we put into understanding them we need to appreciate their complexity and to interpret them in a way that gives us as dreamers the most effective explanation possible.

When we consider a dream in its entirety, we can decide whether the theme of the dream is related to our private and personal lives, our work lives, how we manage relationships, or our emotions, fears and doubts – or whether perhaps there are issues that are more subtle than any of these. What the dream may actually be doing is telling us our basic story – what

we feel instinctively is appropriate action or conduct. We have simply not yet brought that story into conscious awareness.

THE HERO'S AND THE FOOL'S JOURNEYS

The journey to maturity we all experience – beloved by the mythologist and writer Joseph Campbell (1904–1987) and called by him the monomyth (basic story) or the Hero's Journey – follows a very clear path to full understanding and spiritual awareness. Interestingly, pre-dating Campbell's understanding of this quest, the Major Arcana of the Tarot had set out – through the use of rich imagery – the Fool's Journey. This, as we have seen, guides the innocent through a number of rites of passage and initiations, very similar to that put forward by Campbell.

Both of these explorations of the journey from youth to maturity at first glance appear to be male-oriented. Campbell himself said that the heroine was the prize awaiting the hero. The Tarot images were based initially on an understanding of the then somewhat patriarchal world. They were later beautifully enhanced by a 20th-century understanding of symbolism. When the art of creative dreaming is brought into the equation, we have a wonderful synthesis of association, imagery and symbolism.

When these journeys are understood as a search for the hidden aspects of ourselves that we fear and yet must respect, they become non-gender specific. The androgynous Fool learns to balance drive and sensitivity and to pursue initiation at each stage as reward for a grasp of what is newly perceived meaning. Only then can the various thresholds be crossed so that the final goal of illumination can be reached.

The hero on his mythological journey must pass certain tests and overcome various obstacles before he returns home a wiser man, with the added boon of an 'elixir' or blessing that will be of assistance to others. Woman, in the main, is geared towards caring and nurturing. So, when she undertakes a similar quest, the prize is

a full understanding of her own power enhanced by the gift of logic, rationality and clarity of perception.

Obviously our primary concern is with ourselves as dreamer. Dreams are our key to our own individual mythology – our cache of information and ideas – and personal or private concerns. Dreams are highly subjective, so we do have to consider what role we play in the dream. We may be playing an active part, observing the action of the dream, or other dream characters may be affecting our emotions and responses. We may also be aware that we are being watched. Whether we think of ourselves as a Hero full of derring-do or as an innocent Fool does not matter; we shall always gain from the exploration.

The narrative of a dream is the story that it tells us so that we can bring information into conscious awareness. Each dream is its own mini journey,

giving us at that stage the protection, assistance and clarity we need to eventually reach fulfilment. A dream may also be taken as a small reflection – a snapshot or thumbnail picture – of a particular stage of our 'greater journey', whether we are crossing the threshold into some new experience, undergoing a test or initiation, reaching a climax or 'final battle', or even attempting to return to some kind of normality.

This approximates to the idea of both the Hero's and the Fool's Journey when they set out with little idea of what they will discover. On this very personal journey we must as dreamers:

- Learn what is our place in the dream scenario – our role.
- Understand the world in which we find ourselves – our interaction with our environment and with others.
- Learn how to function effectively and comfortably within that world – how to apply the knowledge we gain.

Our exploration of our dream story will inevitably bring some happiness, a number of obstacles and difficulties, and some new understandings of who we are. Ultimately, in common with the Hero and the Fool, we as dreamers return to everyday waking life and bring back a prize (enhanced personal awareness) that enables us to help others in their own quest for knowledge.

THE JOURNEYS COMPARED

The common ground between the Hero's Journey and the dream world is the point at which the Hero has crossed the threshold into the unknown. In dreams, the need to explore or understand that which has seemed weird or strange is the call to adventure, the granting of help and a protective device – as in the Hero's Journey. In the Hero's Journey, supernatural help has been offered in the form of a protective being, amulet or weapon. In the Fool's Journey this protective being appears as the Magician, the need to understand the tools available to us. For a man the 'call to adventure' is often to find his personal Holy Grail or elixir, while for a woman the motivation is more likely to be to rescue a loved one.

Entering a darker unknown world, the tests in the Hero's Journey are often encounters with forces of nature, warriors, sorcerers and monsters – all figures easily recognizable within the dream world. We as Hero/dreamer now begin to understand ourselves and our abilities better; we gain more power over those things that have previously terrified us. In the Fool's Journey, as we follow the Major Arcana, this power is shown to us as we learn more about the intrinsic balance between masculinity and femininity, youth and wisdom. These qualities are pictured in the High Priestess, the Empress, the Emperor and Hierophant, moving from untutored intuition through nurturing and caring, authority and finally into spiritual perception.

At this point we need more assistance. In the Hero's or Heroine's Journey a loyal, or sometimes supernatural, figure may appear; in dreams we recognize that part in ourselves which supports and guides us – perhaps a totem animal, wise friend or the gods and goddesses; in the Fool's Journey we come to understand the Lovers, the integration of masculine drive and feminine intuition. All of these – supernatural figure, wise guide or inner trust – will be with us as we progress to the next stage of our journey.

At the next stage the Hero is offered choices. He meets the Goddess – the epitome of everything that is female – as woman and temptress. He can choose to stay with her or to continue his journey; thus he begins to comprehend the true power of love. The Heroine comes to understand her own drives and power. She learns to confront her own perception of the masculine by understanding her relationship with her father, who often presents as being without power – she must leave him behind. If she is strong enough she will bring about an integration or 'sacred marriage' with her inner masculine. In dreams, we come to a place where we can let go of many of our preconceived ideas and confront our misperceptions. In common with the Fool, we can continue on our journey, balancing the polarities we have so far encountered. We drive the Chariot with skill and attention, understand our own Strength and recognize the Hermit who learns to be alone.

Now there comes a critical point. If the Hero has elected to continue his journey and not to be seduced by Love, he must fight a final battle. His adversary may be perceived as a monster, wizard or warrior, whom he must ultimately destroy: that is his old self. The Heroine confronts her own darkest destructive side, her Shadow, while the Fool comes to understand the turning of the Wheel of Fortune (or Wheel of Life), true Justice and, in the Hanged Man, the making sacred of all he believes in. Dreams, at this point, are a kaleidoscope of images, actions and reactions that highlight our individual concerns and learning. Some dreams may be in explanation, some directional, some full of the imagery of the Tarot or our own beloved myths and fairytales, others frightening and amusing in turn as we sort out our confusion.

With the winning or appropriation of the elixir that he has been searching for, the Hero now starts his flight for home, after seeking atonement with his father. Now he understands his own Ego and those traits of character he has inherited. The Heroine in turn seeks atonement with her mother and, in doing so, understands for the first time perhaps the triple nature of woman – maid, mother and crone. Dreams are now centred on integration, assimilating in a coherent form all that has been learned. For there is further, more subtle, information to be included. It is here that the Fool begins to come into his own, for he too has faced the Death of the old self, along with fear and temptation in the Devil and the Tower. If he remains true to himself and the teachings of the Major Arcana, as shown particularly in the card of Temperance, which signifies refinement, he has a clear path forward guided by his own Star.

As he comes to an appreciation of his own emotions in the card of the Moon and the joy that the new life of the Sun brings, the Fool prepares for a return to the normal everyday World, knowing that he is protected from harm by his own clarity of perception. The Hero, meanwhile, also returns to the ordinary world. This return is sometimes achieved by assistance from that world, sometimes accomplished by his own efforts. Either way, rebirth and resurrection are inherent in his return. The Heroine by now has reached a true realization of her own femininity. She recognizes her power over life and death and is no longer afraid of either. Our own dreams, when we reach this stage, are full of new life and promise. We can look forward with hope and can make better use of our Dream Oracle.

When we develop for ourselves a way of understanding our dreams, perhaps using the symbolism of the Hero's and the Fool's Journey, we make use of all the information they contain. Here the most frequently appearing dream imagery has been categorized, employing the same system as that used in studying the Major Arcana. By using this same system, you too will be able to read the narrative of the dream, absorb the information it contains and finally apply that information within your waking life.

SETTINGS AND SCENERY

Much of the imagery to do with places and environments in dreams is easily interpreted simply by thinking about what that environment means to us. It may suggest a particular mood or feeling we experience in our day-to-day lives in those circumstances; being out in the open air, for example, will feel quite different from being in a factory or busy office, or in our own kitchen. Given that background, particular locations also have archetypal associations, which we have outlined in this section. It also includes background images that have important significances in dreams, such as the weather and the time, and the incidence of numbers, shapes and patterns, which can be very revealing.

PLACES AND ENVIRONMENTS

Highly atmospheric, the environment of our dream can provide a framework for the images by establishing the mood of the dream and therefore of our state of mind.

THE IMAGERY

The *countryside*, for instance, can suggest a feeling of freedom. To be in a *farmyard* in a dream shows us as being in touch with the down-to-earth side of ourselves. An *open-air market* represents a kind of halfway point between a country and urban environment. An *urban environment* or *industrial landscape* may well suggest stress and hard work or bustle and hurry. A *city* or *town* will signify an industrious frame of mind. When we dream of being in a *nightclub* we are highlighting the right of every human being to belong.

Often the setting will echo our everyday concerns, perhaps being similar to our *place of work* or a place that is *easily recognizable*, such as a cemetery. The former might suggest that we need to take note of what is happening in our everyday environment. The latter would not always be to do with an actual physical death, but perhaps the final stages of a particular period in our lives. A *funeral* might indicate that we require a period of mourning for something that has happened in the past. This will then allow us to move forward into the future. Both cemeteries and funerals can also depict our thoughts and feelings about death and the attitudes and traditions surrounding it.

When the dream takes place in a *bank or similar institution* it highlights our financial management; in a *shop* we should perhaps consider the value we place on the services we offer others. Both of these images may also suggest our emotional resources, such as self-confidence, social ability and wisdom. A *pawn shop*, interestingly, would also highlight our efficient use of resources, though it is more to do with the idea of exchanging something of value rather than monetary wealth.

When we become conscious of our environment being a particular room,

such as a lounge, bedroom or kitchen, the personal relevance will be worth interpreting. A *lounge*, for instance, might be a place where we welcome others, a *bedroom* a place of relaxation and a *kitchen* a place of nurturing.

THE SIGNIFICANCE

Often the setting or environment in a dream can give an insight into our state of mind. By looking very carefully at the setting we are in we can often gain additional information as to the relevance of the dream to everyday life. Interpreting the attributes of certain places as they appear in dreams gives us a perception of our own 'inner landscape'.

Thus, a *landscape* that becomes *fertile or lighter* in the course of the dream suggests that circumstances around us may be changing for the better. *Dreary, unfriendly landscapes*, or *tranquil, beautiful places* may well refer to our own subjective view of the world at that particular time. A *particularly dark and depressing atmosphere* can demonstrate the feelings that we have about a situation without necessarily being able consciously to express them. It might also perhaps be a warning or threat that our unconscious self has picked up and not been able to quantify. *A bright airy space* can suggest happiness and potential, and may also be a representation of our own way of looking at life in general.

Places that are familiar to us will evoke certain moods and memories. When details have changed in the dream it perhaps depicts an adjustment in our appreciation of that particular memory. For instance, in dreams, *a childhood home or where we were born* suggests a secure space. However, if it now feels oppressive, it does not seem to be a sanctuary and we may no longer need such safety and reassurance.

A place that seems familiar and yet at the same time appears unknown suggests that there is a situation in waking life that is following an old pattern of behaviour. However, it has unknown elements within it which may help us to develop a different way of reaching a solution. *Unknown or unfamiliar places* usually represent aspects of a situation in waking life that have not yet made themselves apparent.

Characteristics within us that are too frightening or powerful to be allowed full expression in waking life are often perceived in dreams as *enclosed spaces*. *A space sheltered from the elements* offers a degree of peace and tranquillity and may be an initial representation of the still, calm centre within. This calmness can also be represented by dreams of *outer space*, as we widen our perceptions. To be *lost in space* is an experience of the Void (see page 76), which need not be scary if we accept that we can go beyond our own perceived limitations. *Wide open spaces* offer us freedom of movement, and perhaps a sense that we can make the best use of opportunities.

SUBSIDIARY IMAGES AND ASSOCIATIONS

When we begin to pay attention to detail in dreams it can reveal some surprising facts. To dream of being *alone in a desert*, for instance, signifies a lack of emotional satisfaction, loneliness or perhaps isolation; yet it can also be a place of contemplation, quiet and divine revelation. An *oasis* would have this particular significance. *Sand* in a dream would most likely

suggest instability and lack of security, so when the *sands are shifting* we are probably unable to decide what we require in life. *Building sand castles* would indicate that the structure we are trying to give to our lives does not have permanence and may be illusory. To be *on a beach* rather than a desert shows our awareness of the boundary between emotion and reality, and our ability to be in touch with the elements.

We often need a sense of space to make the best use of opportunities or to escape from or leave a situation. We should be capable of going beyond our own concepts of limitation and ego states. In dreams this will often manifest in images of disembarkation points such as *airports and stations or piers and harbours*. We are perhaps travelling towards something new. *Going or being abroad* also has this same significance.

Closer to home, when we become aware of the specific room that we occupy in dreams, we learn to understand just how clever the mind is at presenting information. The different *rooms and parts of houses* indicate the diverse aspects of our personality and experience. For example:

Dreaming of being in an *attic* highlights past experiences and old memories as well as our spiritual leanings and aspirations. The *cellar* most often represents the subconscious and those things we may have suppressed through our inability to handle them. Often containing long-held family beliefs and habits,

particularly those that we have internalized without realizing it, a *basement* can also highlight the power and passion that is available to us in waking life. The *bedroom* portrays a place of safety where we can relax and shut out the outside world. As a place of rest and relaxation, we are able to let go of everyday concerns and perhaps return to an inner state of peace. It being a space where we get rid of unwanted material, the *bathroom* may also suggest a cleansing away of negativity.

Being the 'heart' of the house, the *kitchen* is often the place where the family comes together. In dreams, therefore, it often represents the Great Mother in her role as nurturer. Old-fashioned *larders* and modern *refrigerators* can also symbolize the nurturing function and that of conservation. Hestia, Greek goddess of the hearth, was worshipped using rituals that were originally associated with cooking. The rituals associated with the hearth and with fire were, and still are, a significant part of spiritual development.

BUILDINGS AND STRUCTURES

This section deals with the recognizable buildings and structures most likely to appear in dreams, as well as the integral parts built at the same time as the main structure.

THE IMAGERY

Buildings and other structures that appear in dreams will, by their very nature, call for different interpretations. A *workplace or office* situation is slightly more formal than our home, and highlights our feelings about, or our relationship with, work and authority. Needing some kind of order, bureaucracy or hierarchy to function effectively, its appearance in a dream can also draw attention to issues of relationship, control and management of emotions. More specifically, a *warehouse*, when it is both a workplace and a place for storage, has the symbolism of being a repository either for spiritual energy or for spiritual detritus. In dreams it can also represent the intelligent use of available resources.

A *library* is an important symbol suggesting the Collective Unconscious available to all humanity and the wisdom and skills that we have accumulated. A *museum*, however, denotes old-fashioned thoughts, concepts and ideas. It can also represent a place where we store our memories. At certain stages of awareness, we may dream of a *university* or *school*. Their appearance signifies the degree of experience and learning appropriate at that point in our waking lives.

Dreaming of working or being in a *laboratory* indicates that we need to be more scientific or ordered in our approach to life. We need to make an objective assessment of what is going on in our lives and consider carefully how best to make use of our talents and particular type of creativity. A *garage or workshop* appearing in a dream may indicate how we store and make use of our own talents. It is the creative, productive inner space from which we produce tangible results.

A *house* most often refers to the soul and our sense of inner sanctuary, from which we can build our lives. In a dream of an *impressive, awe-inspiring house* we are conscious of the Self or the Soul, the 'higher' aspects of ourselves, yet a *small house* suggests we may be seeking security, or perhaps the safety of childhood, without responsibility. Conversely it can mean that we feel trapped by responsibilities in the everyday world.

The *front of the house* portrays the façade we present to the outside world, whereas the various rooms (which are explained in Places and Environments on page 89) indicate the diverse aspects of our personality and experience. If *several different activities are going on* at the same time – particularly very diverse ones – it suggests rivalry between two aspects of our personality, possibly the creative and the intellectual, or perhaps the logical and intuitive.

Any *religious building* will suggest a place of sanctuary and refuge, where we may be at peace with our beliefs and raise our own vibration to a more spiritual level. As a place where the Divine resides, such a building in the ordinary world is built to honour and reflect the beauty of heaven. It is a microcosm (small picture) of what is, after all, infinite. This space is one that has been made sacred by the power with which it is invested – usually blessed or consecrated – according to the beliefs of its users. Through dreams and meditation we are capable of developing such an inner space, a place of sanctuary that allows us to let the outside world go and be ourselves.

In dreams, a *church* or a building predominantly associated with a specific religion, such as a *synagogue, mosque or temple*, will focus on the external recognizable aspects of that particular system of belief. It gives the dreamer the

opportunity to crystallize their own feelings about aspect of that faith.

Additionally, in dreams a *temple* can signify our own body, something to be treated with reverence and care. A *tabernacle* tends to be a more temporary structure, or a portable repository for a sacred much-loved object. As such it represents our core belief, carried with us at all times. Many dreams contain images of space underground, and to dream of a *crypt, catacomb or tomb* signifies a need to come to terms with subconscious fears or feelings connected with death. Such a dream may also bring to light concealed religious beliefs and an awareness of hidden mysterious power and the occult. If there are *bodies in the tomb or crypt*, these usually represent parts of ourselves we have either not developed or have suppressed in some way.

A *hospital*, depending on our attitude to such places, may be a place of safety or perhaps one where we feel threatened and vulnerable. It is a healing, perhaps transitional environment or space, where matters physical, emotional or spiritual can be brought into a state of balance. *A hotel, guesthouse or bed and breakfast* place will also represent a transitional space, a place of temporary respite where we can be nurtured and cared for.

A *lighthouse* is a beacon, often bringing a blinding flash of inspiration. As such it can lead us into calmer waters, emphasizing the correct course of action to help us achieve our spiritual goals. Also a warning system, it may alert us to potential emotional difficulties. A lighthouse can also take on the symbolism of a tower.

An image of a *tower* of any sort in a dream represents the personality and the Soul within. While there are obvious connotations that connect it to masculinity and assertiveness, it is perhaps more accurate to perceive it as the Self within the world in which we live. Since the building of a tower, particularly the *steeple of a church*, was initially designed to 'point to the heavens', the symbolism also indicates greater understanding of the Spiritual Self.

On a more mundane level a tower in a dream will often represent a construction that we have developed in our lives. This may be an inner attitude or outer behaviour. A *square tower* signifies a practical approach to life, whereas a *round tower* is more spiritually geared. A *round tower at the end of a square building* is the combination of the practical and spiritual.

Any defended private space such as a *castle, citadel or fortress* may variously represent the feminine nature, a place of safety or our innermost intuitive self. It will sometimes suggest a fairytale or myth-like element in our perceptions. If the structure has *four walls* then mundane or practical considerations are of prime concern. In addition, if the building has a moat, the suggestion is that we are using our emotions in a purely logical way as a spiritual defence rather than allowing them to flow freely. This may be an obstacle in our attempts to access our inner power.

Prison or imprisonment of any sort in dreams stands for the traps we create for ourselves, usually through a sense of duty or guilt. A *barred window or door* in a prison would suggest that we are being prevented from using external resources to their best advantage.

To be in a *public house* in a dream and especially aware of our behaviour indicates how we relate to groups and what our feelings are about society. As a public place where shared values are important, the public house can be a creative space. As a meeting place where few judgements are made, it becomes a place in which people can co-exist.

Because of its geodesic shape, the *igloo* in dreams represents completeness and sanctuary and, by association, the feminine principle. More mundanely, it may represent an apparently cold, uncaring attitude with a hidden warmth.

The *pyramid* is one of the oldest constructions known to man, and is a very powerful image. In the physical realm it is a building that creates awe; mentally it symbolizes regeneration. The true point of power is considered to be in the centre of the pyramid, indicating our own inner potential. Thus, from a spiritual perspective, the pyramid is a guardian of power.

When a building in dreams is in *ruins* we have to ascertain if it is through our own neglect or foolhardiness. If, however, the cause appears to be others' vandalism, we may be making ourselves vulnerable.

THE SIGNIFICANCE

Buildings in dreams generally are symbolic of the structures we build around us to help us manage our everyday lives. The attitudes and beliefs we have formed over the years from our own experiences and perceptions can appear as buildings or parts of buildings; a childhood house might, for instance, suggest a return to innocence or trigger memories that are relevant.

The beliefs and perceptions of others round us, such as our families and close associates, also play a part in those inner constructs that appear in our dreams. The surrounding environment in dreams will often also give us information that reflects our character, hopes and concerns. Just as in waking life we learn a lot about a person from their personal surroundings, we can learn a great deal about ourselves through our dream constructions. Home, after all, is more relaxed than a work environment, the former highlighting personal concerns, the latter our more public persona.

Sometimes in dreams buildings can become composite – containing more than one element to be considered. To understand the relevance of composite images, we should interpret the main appearance of the building first, then the subsequent images as characteristics to be recognized and incorporated into our interpretation.

SUBSIDIARY IMAGES AND ASSOCIATIONS

While the main building is obviously of primary importance, other parts of the structure may also have relevance. In interpreting the deeper meanings of what we are perceiving, the external appearance may provide additional information as also will particular aspects of the internal structure.

Thus, *doors* from a psychological viewpoint can also suggest how we allow people to approach us, and how vulnerable we can become. They may also represent a change of perspective.

Windows will often signify the way that we ourselves view life. Dirty windows will indicate a jaundiced view of life, whereas a *broken* one would suggest a traumatic event.

Passages usually represent a transitional state in life, such as between childhood and puberty. When health matters become a concern, a passage in a dream may sometimes represent one of the bodily functions. A *hallway to the front door* signifies how we respond to the outside world.

A *balcony*, particularly with a balustrade, indicates both support and protectiveness. Psychologically we are searching for a more objective viewpoint, spiritual competence (clarity of perception) or a higher status. Without any kind of surround, a *ledge or sill* may suggest danger of some sort.

Stairs in dreams are often an indication of the steps and effort we must take in order to achieve a goal. A *golden staircase* in dreams is such an iconic image, associated by many people with death, that special attention needs to be paid to other aspects of the dream. As a 'stairway to heaven' and our spiritual aspirations it is the realization that we no longer need to be trapped by mundane concerns but can move towards a more fulfilling life.

In dreams, a *chimney* can indicate how we deal with our inner emotions and warmth of feeling. It may also represent our connection with the Divine – an escape from the mundane and ordinary into freedom. Interestingly, in ancient civilizations, smoke was considered to be a petition to the gods, so any opening in a roof of a temple, tepee or tent represented a change to a higher level of consciousness.

Lifts, elevators or escalators in dreams usually indicate how we deal with information from the spiritual and intuitive realms. There is the belief that when asleep we leave our bodies – we experience a change of consciousness. This can, in dreams, be reflected by lifts, elevators or escalators. When we dream of *getting stuck in a lift* while descending it suggests too much focus on the material world;

while ascending suggests an inability to understand, or a fear of, spiritual or esoteric matters.

A *wall*, depending on its characteristics, often signifies a block to progress. For example, an *old wall* might suggest a problem or difficulty from the past. A *brick wall*, *rampart or dividing wall* all signify the difference between any two states of reality, perhaps our inner psychological state and the exterior everyday world. To *breach walls*, particularly of a defensive structure (as happens in many myths and fairy stories), suggests a freeing of the essential feminine, which gives us a more intuitive approach to life. It also suggests that we have come to an understanding of our own inner power. When *walls are closing in* on us it is most likely to represent a feeling of being trapped by the way in which we live our lives or by circumstances around us.

Our interactions with the various structures in our dreams can also be very revealing. *Being trapped* in any building, for instance, can represent our difficulty in freeing ourselves from old attitudes. Trying to *enter a building* suggests that we recognize obstacles that have to be overcome. *Going into or coming out of a house* clarifies whether we need to be introverted or extroverted at that point in life. *Being outside a house* depicts our more public side. *Moving to a larger house* implies that there is need for a change in our lives, perhaps to achieve a more open way of life, or even for more emotional space.

Making changes to the structure of a house or repairing it in some way shows that we perhaps need to look at health matters or that personal relationships require attention. We may need to appreciate that a level of damage or decay has occurred in some way in our waking lives. A dream that highlights *construction or demolition* does make us aware of our ability to construct successful lives, yet equally the ability to 'self-destruct' in order to make progress.

Going down into any *underground space*, such as a basement, tunnel or catacomb, represents the need to explore our own unconscious and those things we have so far left untouched. *Climbing* any structure is illustrative of the effort that we must make in order to have access to the more mystical, spiritual side of our being.

One other important aspect of the interpretation of buildings and structures is whether a building is known to us or not. If it is known – such as a former residence or a recognizably *significant building*, for instance the Empire State Building or Taj Mahal – we should consider the bearing it has or had in our waking life. If the building is *unknown*, it is the relevance within the dream structure itself that is of note.

OBSTRUCTIONS AND OBSTACLES

Coming up against any kind of obstruction or obstacle is an extremely common, and often revealing, theme in dreams, referring to an obstacle of some kind in our lives.

THE IMAGERY

Almost invariably this mirrors a situation in everyday life where the obstacle is not necessarily physical but is often an emotional difficulty or more deeply hidden problem that stops us in our tracks spiritually.

A *hole in front of us* will represent a difficult or tricky situation. A *pit, abyss or void*, however, is an aspect of the Unknown which all of us must face at some time or another in our lives. The pit tends to represent an emotional state; previously the abyss or void was thought to represent the Underworld, and therefore the unfathomable – the deep. However it is now better understood as a representation of how we can go beyond our own boundaries or present experience. Experiencing such an image in a dream demonstrates a fear of losing control, of a loss of

identity, or of some type of failure. This fear of failure is a very strong emotion and can often also be represented in dreams by a *precipice or cliff*. This psychologically puts us on edge, or on the edge, requiring acknowledgement of the risks involved.

Barriers perceived in dreams are often self-imposed, more often being thought of initially in terms of 'I can't' rather than 'How do I get round this?' Any barrier – particularly *man-made and temporary*, such as a hurdle – suggests that we are coming up against some kind of restraint in waking life, which may be short-lived. A *barricade*, usually set up by an authority, suggests that there is a certain code of behaviour or recognized sense of order that we must conform to. To be *standing on a border between two countries* shows the need to be making great changes in

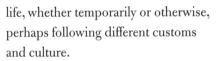

life, whether temporarily or otherwise, perhaps following different customs and culture.

Interestingly, *turning a corner* in a dream can suggest that we have succeeded in moving forward into new experiences, despite what may have seemed to be obstacles in front of us. *Crossing a road* signifies the recognition of danger, fear or uncertainty, though it can also suggest avoidance of such things. *Crossing a river or chasm* often signifies some kind of spiritual adjustment, though not necessarily a physical death. This is a similar interpretation to *standing at a crossroads*, a somewhat magical space, since we can go in any direction that seems appropriate. We are challenged, yet because it is traditionally a space where two opposing forces come together in harmony, we can take time to make the right choices.

Continuing with the concept of movement, many dreams will depict the idea of *climbing a hill or mountain or of reaching a plateau*. The former suggests that we have reached a goal, or a point at which things must inevitably change, and perhaps become easier. In the case of the latter, we have not yet reached the end but can continue on our way without further challenge.

In dreams there are numerous objects or situations that represent obstacles. The object itself can often be relevant, as also can be the particular action or situation that occurs in the dream. A *cell or cage* normally represents some form of entrapment or imprisonment, perhaps of our wilder instincts. We may also be aware of being trapped by the limitations of the physical body, or of being restricted by past experience. Often when we feel trapped in dreams, we are unable to break free of old patterns of thought and behaviour, though these may often be inherited patterns.

A *dam* might represent a sense of frustration or the bottling up of our own emotions whereas a gate can suggest a way through a problem. (Although the 'Pearly Gates' are taken as a symbol of death and the soul's passage to eternity and everlasting life, their appearance in dreams does not usually foretell a death, merely a change of awareness.)

The type of fastening on a closed door or gate will often give us information as to how a difficulty can be overcome. If we are *opening a lock or padlock* we may be trying to open up to new experiences. Both *gates and doors* will signify a threshold experience – being at the commencement of a situation that requires a degree of courage to begin. The threshold experience, or passing through various portals, is a strong one in Masonic imagery and Initiation rites.

THE SIGNIFICANCE

Through dreams we are often able to recognize that there is a problem or an obstacle to progress in waking life. Any obstruction in a dream alerts us to the fact that we cannot, at this stage, reach our goal or achieve a successful outcome. We perhaps have to consider why this is, or even whether the goal itself is appropriate. We must decide whether the obstruction or obstacle has simply arisen of its own accord, whether it has been deliberately placed there either by us or other people, or whether it is an integral part of the dream scenario. This will help us to uncover the root of the problem in everyday life.

There are times when our own inhibitions and anxieties can only be faced when we give them tangible forms. Difficulty, indecision and doubt are three main blocks that occur in life; dreams may give us information as to how we need to tackle the problem. Obstacles in dreams can therefore take on many forms – *a wall, a hill, a dark forest, a pit* and so on. If the obstacle appears insurmountable then we must consciously find our way round it; if it is too difficult to get over, then we may need to use other ways of dealing with what it represents.

SUBSIDIARY IMAGES AND ASSOCIATIONS

If our dream oracle is to work

successfully it must give us clear information, often in symbolic form, as to the nature of the difficulty in everyday life. Ideally, it should also inform us of a potential solution, an action we can take, which we can consciously apply.

Thus in a dream if we are *wearing armour* we may be protecting ourselves, whereas if *others are in armour* we may need to be aware of their defence mechanisms and can adjust our behaviour accordingly. Equally, if we were to be *building a dam* we are also likely to be putting up defences, whereas if a *dam is bursting* we may feel we have no control over emotional situations around us. Once we have identified the image and its relevance to our own circumstances we need to look at what is happening and what interaction is going on.

When we dream of *caging a wild*

Being guarded by another human being suggests the presence of an authority figure in our lives, a representation of an aspect of ourselves that is imposing some kind of control – our own innate sense of law and order. A guard may also represent the Higher Self, or our guardian angel. *Forcing any lock* in order to escape may well indicate that we need not allow ourselves to be trapped.

We have already seen that any kind of hole or pit in dreams helps us to face the unknown, and it is often helpful to look at our own actions. To dream of *falling into a hole* indicates that we are accessing our unconscious feelings, urges and fears. *Walking round it* suggests we are capable of getting round a tricky situation. Interestingly a round hole represents the heavens and the spiritual realms, whereas a square hole represents the Earth and the more mundane. (This has resonance with the explanation for a round tower on page 92.) If we are *digging a pit or hole* we may be creating the difficult situation. If *others are digging the pit,* we are at the mercy of other people. *Pushing someone into a pit* indicates that we are trying to suppress a part of our own personality. If the *pit is bottomless* it signifies that we do not have enough resources to recover a previous situation.

While holes may often obviously be man-made, *plateaux and precipices* tend to be formed naturally, so discovering a plateau might indicate

animal, it is worthwhile looking at how we are accomplishing this and equally what the cage is like. A flimsy cage suggests a less robust approach than a stoutly built one. To be aware of *trapping something or someone* is making an attempt to gain control. To dream that we are in a cage indicates a sense of frustration and perhaps of being trapped by circumstances around us.

that we can legitimately take time out from a situation, or – if it is particularly barren in appearance – that we need additional stimuli before we can move on. A *precipice or cliff* will, in many ways, have the same meaning as a hole, but be potentially more dangerous and need more careful negotiation. The Fool in the Tarot, interestingly, seems unaware of the danger he may be facing.

Gates and crossings usually signify some kind of transition that is occurring, and particularly in the case of the former it is worth taking note of which way it opens. Like doors, if they open away from us it indicates the potential for stepping forward into new experience, if towards us it suggests that we may be aware of the potential but not yet quite ready to take full advantage of the opportunity offered. These are threshold experiences and can have a similar meaning to dreaming

of being *at a crossroads*. Here though, we can gain information from the way we navigate the choices. To *turn left* can indicate taking the wrong route, though it can also indicate the more intuitive path. To *turn right* can thus obviously mean taking the correct path, but can also mean making logical decisions. Going *straight across* would suggest that we are aware that we can afford to ignore any other way – our actions are literally straightforward.

One final image that might sometimes be taken as a barrier is that

of a *forest or jungle*. Such vegetation, mentioned in the section on Nature, Ecology and Plants (see page 102), is usually recognized as being a threshold symbol. Depending on our own perspective, this can signify coming to terms with the realms of the unknown feminine. It can also represent the courage needed to overcome fear and to rescue the trapped intuitive aspect of our own being. It is an image that often appears in myth and fairytale and is an integral part, as we have seen, of the Hero's Journey.

NATURE, ECOLOGY AND PLANTS

The natural world and its associated cycles and patterns of growth often relate to the nurturing and development of different areas in our own lives.

THE IMAGERY

Vegetation in a dream can often represent the underlying abundance and fertility that is available to us and our capacity for growth. *Cultivated ground*, such as a *garden*, can indicate an area of life where we are nurturing our potential, whereas a patch of *weeds* would suggest a neglected area of our personality. Mental attitudes and old patterns of behaviour that clog us up and do not allow us to move forward can very often be shown in dreams as weeds. For instance, a patch of *brambles* can suggest irritating snags to our movement forwards, whereas *nettles* might represent people actually trying to prevent progress.

If the *plants are simply growing wild*, there is a part of us that needs freedom. If they are grown in *regimented or formal rows* we are overly concerned about other people's views and opinions. In dreams *seeds* represent great potential and latent power. *Grass or turf*, particularly if it is uncut, suggests fresh opportunity. As a marker of time, the traditional *sheaf of corn*, a symbol of consolidation and of binding, will suggest autumn – a time of harvest.

Trees in dreams can have particular meaning. A tree with *wide branches* would suggest a warm, loving personality, whereas a *small, close-leafed tree* would suggest an uptight one. A *well-shaped tree* would suggest a well-ordered person, while a *large, messy tree* would suggest a chaotic being. A *forest* traditionally is frequently a place of testing and initiation, an unknown space and threshold experience, as seen in the Hero's and the Fool's Journey. The *jungle* in dreams is an image belonging to mysticism and fairytales and is also a threshold experience. It can often represent chaos –

either positive or negative. *Evergreen* trees, because of their ability to survive any conditions, signify longevity, immortality and everlasting life.

THE SIGNIFICANCE

The management of our natural resources is a topic that is of prime importance within the framework of our everyday lives. As we become more aware of self-responsibility we also become more conscious of the fact that ecology and our relationship with nature and plants is an issue that goes beyond individual responsibility and that of the community. We become more passionate about the survival of the world as we know it, and show a deeply felt response to the misuse of resources.

Often our dreams will demonstrate such concern and the representations of nature become more significant. *Plants*, for instance, will signify the life force and cycle of life. Because of their process of growth and decay they become a symbol for progressive change. Flowers of any sort can indicate love and compassion. *Bouquets, bunches of flowers, garlands and wreaths* all signify honour to one degree or another. Garlands and wreaths in particular, because they are circular, suggest continuity and sometimes commitment.

As more people become aware of ecological issues and children in particular internalize the need for the responsible use of resources, dreams about *ecology* demonstrate a passion for the world in which we live.

SUBSIDIARY IMAGES AND ASSOCIATIONS

Part of natural growth requires the combination of the elements of Earth, Fire, Air and Water. *Mud* – a combination of earth and water – in dreams represents the fundamental substance of life which, handled properly, has a tremendous potential for growth. However, handled badly it can be treacherous. *Quicksand*, a similar combination, signifies a lack of security. *Marshes and swamps* will represent uncertainty. Perhaps we are creating emotional difficulties for ourselves – or even having them created for us – which make it difficult for us to find stability or feel particularly secure.

Many plants have both healing and magical qualities that become apparent in dreams. The *acorn*, for instance, represents prosperity as well as new beginnings; the *daisy* is a recognizable symbol of spiritual purity and joyfulness. A garden full of *many different types of plants* might suggest a form of Paradise. *Mistletoe* is said to represent the essence of life, and is a divine healing substance. *Holly and ivy* are much associated with Christmas or yuletide in Western tradition. Their true significance – following the pagan tradition – is that holly symbolizes holiness, consecration, peace, goodwill and health; ivy meanwhile symbolizes immortality, constant affection and eternal life.

In dreams where a *forest or jungle* appears we often have to look at the interrelationship between the vegetation and ourselves. *Creepers* would suggest that something is trapping us. *Finding a clear space* would suggest that there is a safe space available to us no matter what happens. If we recognize certain trees, for instance, we decide what relevance that has in our everyday life. More specifically, becoming aware of the components of a tree can have the following significances.

The *roots* of a tree are said to show our connection between ourselves and the earth. *Spreading* roots would indicate a degree of extroversion, whereas conversely *deep-rootedness* would suggest a more self-contained attitude. The *trunk* of the tree shows how we use the energies available to us, and also what exterior we present to the world. Thus a *rough trunk* suggests a 'rough and ready' personality, whereas a *smoother trunk* would indicate a level of sophistication. *Branches* signify the stages of growth we go through, and *leaves* suggest the way we communicate to the rest of the world. To be *climbing the tree* suggests we require a sense of perspective or achievement.

One natural form that appears frequently in dreams is the *shell*. As a symbol of mothering it is very important. It can also be seen as a magical symbol that holds within it the power of transformation, whether it is the conch shell as in the Horn of Plenty, or the scallop shell associated with the birth of Aphrodite. The shell shape is the epitome of natural form.

The *spiral* form of many shells suggests the principle of involution and evolution – going inwards towards a central point and coming outwards from that point. It signifies our ability to protect ourselves and our more vulnerable parts. The shell's appearance in dreams may well alert us to the need to protect our own environment.

One particular part of nature that does have significance in dreams is weather. Because its relevance at first glance is not always easily recognizable it does require consideration in its own right, so we have examined this in a later section (see page 118).

NUMBERS, SHAPES AND PATTERNS

Each of us has an instinctive appreciation of the esoteric meaning of numbers and, with a little study, can enhance the interpretation of our dreams by using that knowledge.

THE IMAGERY

With very little difficulty, albeit with some practice, we can tap into our awareness of the esoteric meaning of numbers and can allow our dreams to inform our actions in everyday life. We can begin to understand mathematical principles and ideas that may seem beyond our normal level of comprehension.

Numbers, or natural numbers as they are now called, are those that are used for counting. The words one to nine with the addition of the word zero to represent no-thing were the first to be used. Only when certain symbols (known as numerals – 1, 2, 3 etc.) were attached to these words so that they could be written down did true mathematics really begin to be understood.

Such Arabic numbers had, in fact, been developed from an earlier Buddhist notation called Brahmi numerals dating from the 1st century CE (see information panel opposite).

When what became known as the Hindu Arabic system of numbering (still the most widely used today) began to be employed, ideas such as two representing the concept of duality or polarity became understandable. More philosophical ideas were experimented with and the symbolism was extended to bring about the art of numerology (the study of the occult, hidden or esoteric significance of numbers).

Numbers naturally led to the science of measurement. There is within that field a branch of measurement called sacred geometry. This might also be called the measurement of perfection, for it is thought to mirror the natural laws of creation (see page 109 for just how important pattern and patterning is in nature). This is also why religious buildings of all sorts – *churches*, *temples* or *mosques* – show some aspect of this measurement of proportion, that is, the relationship of the part to the whole.

Over time certain shapes, patterns and Platonic Solids have acquired a symbolic meaning. As we become more proficient at connecting with our Dream Oracle they appear more often and become more personally relevant.

The *dot* symbolizes the central point, from which everything starts. In relation to patterning, it is the point from which the pattern grows. The *circle* is a two-dimensional representation of unity and perfection, the inner being or the Self. With a *dot in the centre* it can signify the soul in completion, and is also the astrological symbol for the Sun. In many ways the *sphere* is the simplest and most perfect of forms, a three-dimensional solid. Usually appearing as a globe or ball, in dreams it suggests perfection and completion of all possibilities.

The *oval* is formed by the intersection between two interlinking circles. It symbolizes where the spiritual and physical worlds meet – a very powerful energized space. Associated with the Moon, the *crescent* represents the feminine, mysterious power that is intuitive and non-rational. It may be shown as either waxing (becoming larger) or waning (growing smaller).

The *spiral* is symbolically the perfect path to evolution. The principle is that everything is continually in motion, but also continually rising up or raising its vibration. The *labyrinth* is a slightly more complex figure than the spiral. The route in one type is 'unicursal' – that is, it goes by a straightforward route that covers maximum ground straight to the centre and out again. Both the *maze*, and the second type of labyrinth, are designed with the intention to confuse, and have many blind alleys and unexpected twists. In traversing the labyrinth many trials and tribulations are met and overcome or negotiated on the path to attainment undertaken by the Fool and the Hero.

The *triangle* can be a representation of the family – mother, father and child – but probably more often symbolizes Upright Man, with his three parts – body,

BRAHMI AND ARABIC NUMERALS
We can clearly see the similarity between Brahmi numerals and the way we form numbers today.

1	—
2	=
3	≡
4	+
5	h
6	ϥ
7	ʔ
8	ら
9	ʔ

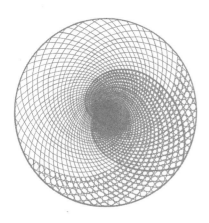

mind and spirit (or being). Through his sheer physicality, there is potential still to be realized. A *hexagram* is a geometric figure that signifies the harmonious development of the physical, social and spiritual elements of human life. Beautifully illustrated in a honeycomb, it symbolizes integration into a perfect whole.

The *square* signifies the manifestation of spirit into matter. It represents the earthly realm as opposed to the heavens. A *square within a circle* suggests the act of 'becoming'. When a human figure is shown within the square it represents Perfect Man. As a solid object, the *cube* signifies mundane concerns, stability and physical manifestation. In dreams it will appear when we need to be entirely practical and focused in our approach. The *Ka'aba* (Arabic for cube) houses the black stone sacred to Islam.

The *cross* is one of the most common structures in Western cultures. The stem of the cross, the vertical line, stands for the heavenly or spiritual, while the transverse beam represents the material physical plane. It is represented in several forms in the Tarot. It is also known to be a protective device against all forms of evil. A *diamond* shape appearing in a dream indicates that we have options available, some of greater value and some lesser.

The *star*, particularly if it is a bright one, indicates an individual's hopes, aspirations and ideals. It is those things we must reach for. The number of rays a star has will be significant. The pentacle (as seen in the Tarot), for instance, has five rays.

The *swastika* with its arms moving clockwise portrays Ideal Man and the power he has for good. In Eastern symbolism it signifies the movement of the Sun.

THE SIGNIFICANCE

Leonardo Pisano, who lived at the turn of the 13th century, is better known by his nickname Fibonacci. His book *Liber Abaci* (Book of Calculation) was based on the arithmetic and algebra that he had accumulated during his worldly travels. It was he who introduced the Hindu-Arabic place-valued decimal system and the use of the nine Arabic numerals into Europe.

The *Fibonacci numbers* and fractals have huge significance in the understanding of numbers and numbering, if only because the ability to count and the patterns in nature are largely based on these two principles. At some point or another they almost certainly will appear in dreams or in meditation.

Broadly, the Fibonacci sequence starts with 0, 1, 1, 2 and continues by adding together the previous two numbers, thus $1 + 2 = 3$, $2 + 3 = 5$, $3 + 5 = 8$, $5 + 8 = 13$, $8 + 13 = 21$ and so on *ad infinitum*. Many mathematical theories follow, and are solved by, the simplicity of this sequence. From this sequence was also calculated what has come to be known as the golden mean or ratio.

Discovered by the Greeks and incorporated into their art and architecture, this is a unique ratio (or relationship between parts) that reoccurs over and over as the most efficient geometry – measurement – for natural growth, energy conservation and beauty.

It was only when computers that had the capacity for massive calculations were developed that another aspect of this inherent patterning was perceived. This was the understanding of what has come to be known as *fractals* – complex geometric patterns. Fractals, as with the golden mean, are found throughout nature. They are present in inorganic structures such as clouds and coastlines and in living structures – even in unexpected places such as the circulation or intestinal systems in mammals.

Often in dreams what appears to be totally chaotic actually has an inherent sense of order, and it is this ordering that is perhaps most important. Many creative projects can be initiated from repeating patterns that first appear in dreams and then are further contemplated in meditation and creative visualization.

It is this similarity and patterning that ultimately gives us the esoteric symbolism of numbers. Almost all ancient systems recognized the significance and power of numbers, both as single digits and, when combined in particular ways, even more powerful figures. They could also be used to signify something else – a kind of code that could hide information from those who were not privy to it and reveal it to those who were.

Today we are able to discover those codes through the use of number and numerology. Because Tarot is based on the Kabbalah, which itself uses a numerical code, we can obtain deeper meaning from the information we receive from numbers. In the section on the Minor Arcana (see pages 64–67), brief interpretations of some of the meanings of number are given. When we add dreaming – along with our own personal library of symbols and meaning – into the equation we can come to an even deeper understanding of our own reactions and responses to life.

At a certain stage of development on our personal journey, the geometric shapes that will give us a greater understanding of the abstract world begin to appear spontaneously in dreams and meditation. It is as though we have broken through, or opened, a door to a new understanding. Our old perception of form is beginning to take on a new meaning and interpretation, to become more sacred. We are able to begin to perceive the deeper, more esoteric, meaning in articles around us in the everyday world.

The patterns that appear as part of the scenario in dreams can categorize how we handle the patterns and perhaps repeated behaviours in our lives. In some patterns, the basic figure that is repeated over and over again draws our attention to the significance of numbers and the symbolism of shape. The patterns that are

repeated in nature, such as the patterning on snakes or the repeated regularity of ferns as they grow, are in their own way small miracles of creation. As we come to have greater access to our own creativity we learn to accept the nature of things as they are. We can look at the fundamental structure of our own natures; we can appreciate the basic shape our life is taking without placing emotional inhibitions in the way.

SUBSIDIARY IMAGES AND ASSOCIATIONS

It has long been accepted that by combining numbers in certain ways, influence can be brought to bear on our environment and on our sense of wellbeing. As we progress on our journey we become more able to make the best use of the subtle vibratory effects of numbers.

Not everyone will necessarily wish to know the ins and outs of the art of numerology. First considered frightening and incomprehensible, numbers were later found to be highly significant in understanding some universal truths. Those basic meanings still resonate with us in the modern world.

The art of numerology today has taken on fresh meaning as we relearn to use numbers in the old ways. In Hebrew, in what is known as *geomatria*, each letter possessed a numerical value and so became a valuable code to hide information from the uninitiated. We are now able to calculate the numerical equivalence of letters, words or phrases, and thus gain insight into different concepts and to explore the interrelationship between words and ideas. Pythagorean numerology, as it has become known today, however, actually has nothing to do with Pythagoras the philosopher except to base itself on his principle of numbers being symbols for ideas.

Once the basic symbology of numbers is accepted, there is further information that can be gained from the use of shape. Under a religious prohibition on depicting life-like figures, Islamic artists designed many abstract decorations based on tessellation. Tessellations are regular patterns of tiles that cover surfaces without overlapping or leaving any gaps. In dreams we frequently perceive such patterns without truly appreciating their significance.

Such patterns were genuinely offering homage to the Divine. Other geometric shapes also offer additional information that 'speaks' to us. The oval, for instance, in religious art, gives us what is called the *Vesica Piscis* or *mandorla*, which is the halo that completely encircles a sacred figure. This is represented in the World card in Tarot.

In symbolism and in dreams it will depend on which way a *triangle* is pointing as to its meaning. If the triangle *points upwards* it represents human nature reaching towards the Divine. If it is *pointing down* it is spirit seeking expression through the mundane. When two triangles meet, as in the *six-pointed star or Star of David*, the physical and the spiritual are joined together in harmony to create wisdom. The *five-pointed star or pentagram* evokes personal magic, and all matter in harmony. The star should point upwards. In dreams it signifies our ownership of our own magical qualities and aspirations. If it is pointing downwards, as seen in the Devil card in the Tarot, it suggests egotism and misuse of power. The eight-pointed star is fully explained as a guiding light in the card of the Star in the Tarot section. *Twelve stars* grouped together are said to symbolize both the Twelve Tribes of Israel and the Apostles.

The *spiral* form and the *labyrinth* are very closely connected. The former becomes more fascinating as we make further progress on our journey. If the *spiral is moving towards the centre* we are approaching our own inner being by an indirect route. A *clockwise outward movement to the right* is a movement towards consciousness and greater enlightenment. If *counter-clockwise*, the movement is towards the unconscious, possibly regressive behaviour. There is also a connection with the navel or solar plexus as the centre of power, known in Eastern martial arts as the *dan tien*.

The *swastika*, associated by many with Nazi atrocities, is actually a very potent symbol, although its representation nowadays is of an entirely negative force. It initially meant wellbeing. Esoterically, *facing right* it symbolizes the evolution of the universe, *facing left* it stands for the involution (descent into matter). It is a good luck symbol for many people in the East, and is considered particularly holy by the Hindu and Buddhist religions. It signifies grounded stability since it points in all four directions (North, East, South and West). When seen in dreams, we would do well to explore our own reactions to it and to decide what our attitude is to its meaning. As so often happens, we may be quite surprised by what information we are being given.

SIGNIFICANCE OF NUMBER

This table is a brief analysis of number significance, showing some traditional meanings. We have included both the numeral and the word, since it has been believed that the word itself resonates at a certain vibration. The Significance column is a broadbrush approach that can be related to dream imagery. For example, a square (or four of anything) appearing in a dream would symbolize stability.

NUMBER	SHAPE	SIGNIFICANCE
0 (Zero)	Cipher	No-thing, the Absolute
1 (One)	Unity	Oneself, the first
2 (Two)	Cross	Balance, opposites
3 (Three)	Triangle	Freedom, triad
4 (Four)	Square	Stability, practicality, manifestation
5 (Five)	Pentagram	Change, action
6 (Six)	Hexagon	Harmony, balance, efficiency
7 (Seven)	Heptagon	Magical forces, spirituality, consciousness
8 (Eight)	Octagon	Infinity, spiritual and physical unity
9 (Nine)	Nonagon	Descent of spirit into the mundane
10 (Ten)	Decagon	Completion, fresh energy

COLOUR

Colour in dreams can be highly significant. It can be true to life or so bizarre as to need interpretation by relating it to our circumstances and to the symbolism of colour.

THE IMAGERY

An example of a bizarre instance of colour might be that a yellow banana would be totally in order whereas a blue one would require quite some consideration. While apparently completely bizarre, a little thought will reveal the meaning. By looking at the Subsidiary Images and Associations below we can see that blue is a healing colour suggesting relaxation. One suggestion therefore for this particular interpretation might be that efforts need be made in waking life to heal a dietary deficiency, which could help sleeplessness or insomnia.

Until the 17th century it was believed that light was colourless, and the laws of refraction and reflection were not well understood. This meant that the use of colour had little symbolism; it was only when it was realized that colour was experienced subjectively did artists and metaphysicists start experimenting and giving colour symbolic meaning. Much of that early symbolism still holds good in our thinking today.

By tradition *black* holds within it the potential for all colours. Rather than being negative, in dreams it suggests absorption and the ability to make use of all available resources. *Blue* is the colour of a clear sky and is also the primary healing colour. *Brown* is the colour of the earth and also represents grounding and stability. *Green* is the colour of nature and of plant life. It also suggests nourishment of the self, particularly of our aspirations and desires. There is probably no true *grey*, only shades of the mixture of black and white, which in dreams will suggest degrees of negativity and positivity. *Magenta* is a colour that links both the material and the spiritual realms. *Orange* is an essentially cheerful, uplifting colour. *Yellow* is the colour that is closest to sunlight, the life-giving force. As a golden colour it suggests prosperity and best use of earthly resources. *Red* suggests vigour, strength, energy, life, sexuality and power. *Turquoise* is a clear greenish blue, which in some religions is the colour of the freed soul. In its iridescent form it will represent,

for many, a kind of spiritual attainment. *Violet*, while found by some to be too strong and rather overwhelming, retains its connection with royalty and means noble actions, especially for the greater good. *White* contains all colours and when passed through a prism gives us the colours of the rainbow. In dreams, this can represent the stages of growth we go through as we reach maturity or progress on our journey.

THE SIGNIFICANCE

Colour now plays a vital part in all symbolism. This is partly to do with ancient traditions and partly to do with the vibratory frequency that each individual colour has. Colour actually affirms the existence of light, and once the colour spectrum was discovered the vibrational energy of the *colours of the rainbow* could be given meaning. Scientific experiments have now been carried out to ascertain what effect colour has, and have proved what occultists and healers have always known: colour can have a profound effect on mood and wellbeing.

In working consciously with the *colours of the rainbow*, we discover that the warm, lively colours – which give back light – are yellow, orange and red. Cold, passive colours are blue, indigo and violet. Green is a synthesis of both warmth and cold. Black absorbs all colour, while white light holds all colour in it. From a spiritual perspective this balance provides a backdrop to the whole of existence.

SUBSIDIARY IMAGES AND ASSOCIATIONS

As we delve deeper into dream significance we will tend to develop our own personal, subjective spectrum of colour. As we become more proficient, we may experience a degree of synaesthesia in dreams, where certain perceptions appear to have a profound effect on our other senses. The shades and hues that we manifest, while corresponding largely to basic meaning, will have a distinct, recognizable vibration. It is for this reason perhaps that some people appear to be fearful of their more bizarre dreams.

Taking a somewhat broadbrush approach, the following, in the same order as above, are the more intrinsic meanings. *Black* suggests manifestation, negativity and a judgemental approach whereas *blue* indicates relaxation, sleep and peacefulness. *Brown* is the colour of commitment and occasionally death. *Green* is the colour of balance and harmony while *grey* represents devotion and ministration. *Magenta*, a particular mixture of red and purple, signifies relinquishment, selflessness, perfection and meditative practice. *Orange* is associated with happiness and independence and clear *red* is appropriate for the qualities of vitality and lust for life. *Turquoise* suggests calmness and purity whilst *violet*, an uplifting colour, evokes respect and hope. *White* suggests innocence, spiritual purity and wisdom. *Yellow* is connected with the emotional self, its attributes being thinking, detachment and judgement.

The stages of growth towards maturity have also been attributed certain colours. Red is the colour of self-image and sexuality; orange is relationship – both with ourselves and others. Yellow is the emotional self, green is self-awareness, blue is self-expression and wisdom. Indigo is the colour of creativity, while violet depicts cosmic responsibility. These are likely to appear spontaneously in dreams as we progress.

POSITION

We can learn much from where things are in relation to us as dreamers, so it is valuable to consider this when looking at the position of characters, articles or environments.

THE IMAGERY

When we dream of anything *higher or above us* our spirit, intellect, ideals and consciences are being brought to our attention. Anything *underneath, below or downstairs* signifies the more mundane concerns and perhaps the most basic issues we have. Being aware of something *behind us* will often highlight the past, as well as suggesting support in the here and now. Something *in front* usually indicates being drawn forward or belonging to our future. Anything to *the right* represents the more dominant logical aspect of our waking self. It is the consciously expressed, confident, more objective side. When we are drawn to *the left* it suggests the less dominant, more passive intuitive aspect of our nature. When we *cannot decide between left and right* it suggests an inability to choose whether to rely on drive or instinct.

THE SIGNIFICANCE

When a particular position is highlighted in a dream it usually signifies our moral standpoint, or our position in life. It can also give an indication of how we are handling situations in our lives. For instance, something in *the wrong position* means we are going about things in the wrong way. If we are aware of anything appearing *upside down* it emphasizes the potential for chaos and difficulty. The 'ups and downs' of situations in life can be experienced in dreams as the actual *movement of our position*. Having our attention drawn to a *backward* movement is usually indicating the potential to adopt a regressive backward-looking tendency. Looking or moving *forward* suggests that we focus on the future. Dreaming of something that is *far away* may indicate that it is far away in time. This may be future or past, depending on other elements of the dream. A *long way in front* would be future, a *long way behind* would be past. *Near or close* would mean recently, or in the immediate.

SUBSIDIARY IMAGES AND ASSOCIATIONS

In the symbolism of the cross in

Number, Shapes and Patterns (see page 108) we discover that the horizontal usually symbolizes the material world and the vertical, the spiritual. This pertains insofar as position is concerned, so for the eye to be drawn *upwards*, for instance, to the top of a building, suggests that we should consider more than just our own ordinary day-to-day concerns. It would be worth considering the effect we have on other people.

When something is on the *same level, but opposite*, us there may be a difficulty in reconciling two ideas or principles, or we may need to understand how others can have an effect on us. Anything *below us* indicates that we most likely have a feeling of superiority. In the Hero's Journey, for instance, were we helping someone to come out of the pit, we ourselves would be aware of the necessity for the gift or boon in the everyday world. In dreams, feeling *lower than our surroundings* can suggest a sense of inferiority or humility.

Often when the *left-hand side* is highlighted in dreams it can be taken to represent all that is dark and sinister and those parts of our personality that we try to suppress. It is more to do with instinctive behaviour, what feels good inside and with personal behaviour without attention to moral codes. The *right-hand side* is more to do with 'rightness' – that is, correctness and moral and social attitudes. Such interpretations will only occur to us after we have begun to look at the more subtle nuances of the ways in which our Dream Oracle communicates with us and will often be dependant on our interpretation of other imagery.

In this same vein, ritual and ceremonial magic, which is now coming back into vogue, both tend to awaken old correspondences, imagery and long-forgotten information. This includes the use of compass direction, long understood by our forefathers. As people become more aware of symbolism through the use of ritual and ceremonial magic, such information will often begin to resurface in dreams.

It will depend on which system of knowledge one wishes to subscribe to, but the original system of correspondences can actually be traced back to Dr John Dee in the 16th century. Society was less scientifically minded and based on intuition. For easy reference each compass direction was allotted an element – either Fire, Air, Water or Earth – and this still pertains today, particularly in regard to Tarot (see information panel).

TAROT SUITS AND ELEMENTS

In the Minor Arcana in the Tarot, each suit is assigned an element and therefore a compass direction. Each element also has a colour correspondence.

COMPASS DIRECTION	ELEMENT	TAROT	COLOUR
North	Earth	Pentacles	Green/Brown
East	Air	Wands	Yellow
South	Fire	Swords	Red
West	Water	Cups	Blue

TIME

With the mind freed from everyday constraints, time is usually immaterial: time in a dream may seem 'over in a flash' or action seem to take place over a long period.

THE IMAGERY

In many ways, however, we are so tuned into diurnal and seasonal rhythms that these do achieve a symbolism in dreams.

To dream of a *dawn* or a *new day* represents a new beginning or a new awareness, usually bringing with it a sense of hope in circumstances around us. The *evening* can be a synonym for *twilight* and the boundaries of our conscious mind. It may also signify old age and wisdom.

Night signifies a period of rest and relaxation. It also symbolizes the darkness that occurs before rebirth or initiation, a fallow period where we gather energy for a new project. It can, however, also suggest a time of chaos and difficulty. Dreaming of *both day and night* indicates the cycle of time or of changes that will inevitably take place. When we become conscious of the seasons of the year in dreams, we are also linking with the various periods of our lives: *Spring* signifies childhood, *Summer* – young adulthood, *Autumn* – middle age, *Winter* – old age.

Images connected with the measurement of time can have particular relevance in dreams. A *clock-face* usually will alert us to the passage of time, a sense of duty or of urgency. An *alarm clock* literally sounds a warning of some sort, while a *digital clock* alerts us to the significance of the numbers shown. An *electric timer*, such as is used to clock in to work, might indicate a measured period of hard work while a *kitchen timer* would suggest nurturing or a creative period ahead. An older symbol like an *hourglass* would initially indicate that time is running out in some way. This image is now frequently seen in computer games, so achieves fresh relevance today. In former times, the hourglass was frequently taken as a symbol of death, as was the figure of *Father Time*. More properly the former is now seen as a symbol for the passage of life, while Father Time represents experience and old age.

THE SIGNIFICANCE

Strictly, because the mind is free from constraints in dreams, time is unimportant. If time is deemed to be significant in a dream, it is usually necessary to measure it in some way. Usually we are only aware of the *passage of time*, or that a particular length of time is meaningful in the dream – it is part of the dream scenario. Dreaming of *something that measures time* often alerts us to the need for us to measure our thoughts and activities.

When we consider dream content, the time may symbolize a particular time in one's life. The *daylight hours* will thus suggest our conscious waking life; where *several days* (or other long periods) seem to pass, some other activity in which we are not involved has been going on. The *hours of the day* could refer to a time in our life or it may simply be the number of the hour that is important, so we should look at the significance of numbers we notice.

SUBSIDIARY IMAGES AND ASSOCIATIONS

When *a particular date* is highlighted in a dream, we are probably being reminded of something highly significant – or possibly traumatic. We may also consider the symbolism contained in the date itself. As we learn more about our own way of operating, the psyche gives us information that is precognitive and may have relevance as we journey through life. Paying attention to this kind of detail can be immensely rewarding in helping to make sense of the information depicted in our dreams.

Recognizing that we have *arrived early* would indicate that we may have to wait for something to happen before we can carry on with our everyday lives. *To be late* might suggest some kind of delay or lack of attention to detail. Both types of dream tend to highlight our personal anxieties. There are some other further interpretations of periods of time that can help clarify a dream (see information panel).

TIMES OF DAY
Specific times of the day tend to have a particular significance.

TIME	SIGNIFICANCE
Morning	The first part of our life or our early experiences
Mid-day	Fully aware and being conscious of our activities (living mindfully)
Afternoon	Putting experience to good use
Twilight or dusk	A period of uncertainty and possible ambivalence. Also a period of transition
Evening	Being more relaxed about life
Night	Being introspective or at rest; also possibly a period of low energy or secrecy
Midnight	A change of pace or of focus

WEATHER

Because the weather is such an integral part of our everyday lives it can go almost unnoticed in dreams, but it often highlights a particular theme or idea.

THE IMAGERY

Storms, thunder and lightning all have an innate connection with the element of fire and are much to do with passion of one sort or another. This could be negative, in the sense of an outburst of aggression and rage, or positive in the sense of a blinding flash of inspiration or some kind of spiritual catharsis. *The Sun*, while also connected with fire, is more connected with the giving of life. *Wind, hurricanes, tornadoes, gales and whirlwinds* are all connected with air. Air represents the intellect or driving spirit, so any of these weather features appearing in dreams suggests a deeply experienced revelation, sweeping all before it and causing a radical change in perspective.

Any *weather condition connected with water* will usually highlight our emotional state. In its simplest meaning, *rain* stands for tears and emotional release. *Hail*, because it is frozen rain, signifies the freezing of our emotions. *Snow*, however, is a crystallization of water, and as such represents the pleasing crystallization of an idea or project. When *melting*, it can represent the softening of the heart and emotions. *Ice* is a representation of rigidity. It is the brittleness that comes from not understanding what is going on around us, of creating circumstances where people cannot get – or be – in touch with us. Existing in isolation because of the way our lives have gone can also be symbolized by *icicles*. A *glacier* or *iceberg* would suggest the inexorable forces of our nature.

An *earthquake* represents some kind of imminent upheaval, perhaps a loss of inner security. On a spiritual level, *an eclipse* can suggest a loss of faith in oneself, but also a sense of being ignored or not noticed. To dream of being in *a fog or mist* marks our confusion and inability to confront, or often even to see, the real issues in our lives. We are often confused by external matters and the impact they may have on us emotionally. A mist may also signify a state of limbo, a transition or a change in awareness.

THE SIGNIFICANCE

Weather, being part of the environment of the dream, usually indicates our moods and emotions. Different types of weather may be symbolic of a deeper inner response to external conditions. Through recognizing the weather conditions in dreams we can become very much aware of changing external situations. We have to be careful to adjust our conduct in response to these. By being forewarned in such a way of external factors, we can develop the ability to control internal moods and emotions that may help us deal with these factors. Being aware of the seasons and the changing weather associated with them draws attention to, in turn, new growth or opportunities, success in projects we have around us, harvesting of our efforts and conservation of energy. Being aware of the weather would also indicate the need to recognize that we are part of a greater whole.

SUBSIDIARY IMAGES AND ASSOCIATIONS

In times gone by, the *forces of nature* were seen to be of supreme importance and, therefore, were often associated with deities. The Norse Forge gods were thought to use thunder and lightning as weapons, as did Rudra the Hindu storm god. The Egyptians chief god was Ra the Sun god, and Ametarasu is a Shinto goddess associated with the Sun. A sunny day in dreams therefore signifies that we are, at that time, particularly blessed.

Both the Romans and Greeks had their corn goddesses, as well as those associated with the harvesting of other crops. Zephyr was a Greek god of the West wind, while Boreas ruled the cold North wind. Indeed most cultures pay due deference to some personalization of weather.

It is easy to see, therefore, why an eclipse was much feared and in dreams is still taken to foretell some kind of misfortune. A rainbow appearing in a dream is the promise of something better to come, however, and any dream that depicts the planets widens our perspective from purely mundane concerns. When we dream specifically of the planet Earth, it highlights our concerns about more global issues as well as our place in the world.

WATER

There are so many aspects to water that it is often necessary to perceive it differently according to its place in the dream.

THE IMAGERY

A *sea* or *ocean* usually depicts total knowledge – the not yet explored. It also represents the Great Unconscious and our emotional connection to The Ultimate, whatever we consider that to be. Being aware of *the tide* in the sea suggests that we need to be more aware of the ebb and flow of life in general and perhaps the passage of time. Indeed, any *current* will highlight the speed with which we live life and with it the potential for change. A *body of water* such as a *lake*, *lagoon*, *pond* or *pool* can signify a stage of transition between the conscious and the emotional self, or alternatively between the latter and the spiritual realms. Interestingly, the domain of the mysterious darker side of the feminine is often pictured as a lagoon in myth and fairytale, as it is in dreams.

Flowing water, such as that in rivers and streams, tends to signify either the surge of our emotions or – quite literally – our ability to 'go with the flow'. *Rivers or streams* themselves symbolize the life we live and the way we live it; in dreams we may perceive life as anything from a large river to a small stream. *Waterfalls* in dreams often suggest some kind of emotional overflow or clearout, perhaps even a spiritual cleansing. *Floods*, in that they can be destructive and bring chaos, signify a major change in our emotional state, the kind of purging that must bring about change in its wake.

Canals as man-made structures can often symbolize the boundaries we impose upon ourselves, attempts to regulate our emotions or, more prosaically, the process of birth. If a *fountain* appears in a dream it will depend on whether it is something natural – like a geyser – or if it is man-made. If the former, it is often representative of a breakthrough in understanding our own emotions. If the latter, it is a channelling of our emotions in order to achieve more mastery over our circumstances. Fountains may also be taken as symbols of womanhood, in particular the Great Mother or, in Tarot, the Empress in her most giving sense.

THE SIGNIFICANCE

Water is usually taken in dreams to symbolize all that is emotional, feminine and intuitive. In that it seeks its own level, but also has movement in its flow, in dreams it can act as a gauge of our emotional state and the flow of emotions – conscious and unconscious. *Deep water* would thus represent a depth of emotion or perhaps the potential for us to be out of our depth in some way; *rushing water* stands for passion, whereas *shallow water* would signify more superficial emotions or those which can be easily handled. Being aware of *the bottom of a body of water* can be seen as a synonym for getting to the bottom of an emotional problem or difficulty. *Clear water* would be understood as clarity of emotion; *murky water* that matters should be allowed to settle.

Water can also represent our hidden potential and, in response to a deep-felt need for change, perhaps represented by a strong current, our ability to create a new life for ourselves.

SUBSIDIARY IMAGES AND ASSOCIATIONS

The subsidiary images associated with water are often explained by an action taken with it or what happens to it. Hence, if we or someone else is *diving* into it we may interpret that as taking some kind of risk or trying to find a suppressed part of our personality.

If we are *drowning* it indicates that we are overwhelmed by emotion, whether our own or someone else's. Realizing that someone else is in the same position suggests we are aware of others' emotional distress. *Walking or jumping into water* symbolizes our need to refresh ourselves or to use our skills in a more intuitive way. To be *in the water while the current swirls* around us although we are not moving suggests a type of inertia. To be *on the water* (for example, in a boat) can suggest that we have not yet decided to make an emotional commitment to something or someone. Seeing our *own image reflected* in water, particularly if the image is distorted, requires us to confront the shadow side of the self – all that we most dislike. *Bathing in water*, even in an action as mundane as taking a bath, suggests cleansing of some sort – as does dreaming of *baptism*. This latter may not have a spiritual connotation at all, but signifies the need for purity and a lack of contamination of ideas in our waking lives.

TAROT ASSOCIATIONS
Here is a list of the Tarot cards in the Major Arcana which have quite prominent representations of water as an integral part of their design.

WATER IMAGE	ASSOCIATED CARD
Sea	Death
Lake	Temperance
Pool	The Star
Flowing water	Temperance
River	The Chariot
	The Moon
Waterfall	The Empress

THE TOWER DREAM

Here is an example of how you can examine the imagery of a particular dream using the dream images outlined in this section and the Tarot card symbolism.

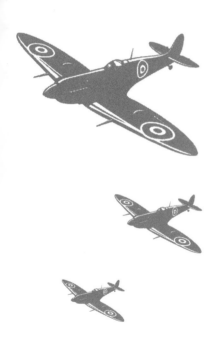

THE IMAGERY

'I am in a nondescript office having a meeting with an ex-boss of mine. Although in some ways I had admired him, we had parted on not particularly good terms some years previously in waking life. There is a definite sense of irritation on both our parts in the dream.

'We are looking out of the window, which makes up almost all of one of the walls. I am struck by how grey and drab the view is, almost industrial in nature with numerous low-level buildings. It is very similar to how Eastern Europe used to be depicted on television.

'I then realize that I am outside flying under my own steam, effectively using my arms as wings. To my right is a short tower block that has a crashed plane on either side of it. The planes have definitely not crashed into the building itself. Although the front part of each plane has crashed into the ground, neither seems to have sustained any other damage. The one on the left is a Royal Air Force Spitfire of Second World War vintage. I can't identify the one on the right but I do notice it is light in colour.

'It seems that the tower block has fallen straight into the ground, but again does not seem to have sustained any other visible damage. There is a lot of white foam around the bottom of both the planes and the building. Strangely, I am not particularly disturbed by the scene, simply acting as an observer.

'I become very aware of a very tall, 1960s-style concrete tower block, directly in front of me, set slightly back from the main scene. For some reason I find this building extremely imposing.

'On waking, I realized I was more disturbed by the dream itself than I was while

actually participating in the dream. In the last part of the dream I was definitely more of an observer.'

THE SIGNIFICANCE

The first aspect that is significant is that the dreamer awakens being aware that she is more disturbed by the dream than she was while in it. This presupposes that some action must be taken when she has worked with the dream and interpreted it.

There are several recognizable themes in this dream. First is that of flying, both by the dreamer herself and also in the symbolism of the planes. Secondly is the representation of the tower blocks – one quite short – from the 1960s. Thirdly is a recognizable time frame set by both the Spitfire and the date of the towers. The indications are that the dreamer has some issues from the past to consider – the only other person in the dream is an authority figure from the past.

ASSOCIATIONS AND INTERPRETATION

Dealing with the last theme first suggests that both the dreamer and her ex-boss are aware of an irritation with one another, possibly an inability to understand the other person. This is a residual feeling from previous experiences that must be dealt with before the dreamer can have the freedom to be objective – to fly, using her arms with a great deal of effort. The wide window suggests that she needs a different perspective, as does the flying. The overall feeling is of drabness, both in the place of work and of struggle in the surrounding environment, from which she needs to be free.

Two attempts at freedom have already come to grief, as symbolized by the crashed planes. One is old-fashioned and associated with war and conflict, perhaps suggesting outmoded methods, while the other is lighter, yet has still crashed. It would seem that it is the working parts of the planes that have been damaged. The foam would suggest that fire has been extinguished. Fire can signify passion, so passion has been extinguished leaving the surroundings intact but drab.

The tower blocks are important in that they give us an image that relates directly to the Tarot. Any tower signifies the way we construct our lives and, in the case of the smaller tower, can be interpreted as a part of the dreamer's life that has not suffered unduly through her attempts to be free of constraints. The other suggests that she may need to return to a previous, perhaps different, set of values in order to fully gain freedom. As she finds the tower imposing, something from that era in her life is colouring her beliefs and actions today. Once she understands this, she will be able to be more dispassionate than perhaps she has been until now. (The dreamer comments that she is not disturbed by the events, but is simply observing, reinforcing the idea that she needs to be more objective.)

FURTHER CLARIFICATION THROUGH THE TAROT

Using the Tower card for clarification suggests that the dreamer must realize that her life needs to undergo some reassessment. The image is of a tower struck by lightning. Its inhabitants are falling out of, or fleeing from, the building. The main structure still stands and yet there is a sense of destruction present.

The lightning suggests some kind of revelation or cataclysmic event that will alter the way life is lived. Old attitudes and ideas must be thrown out and the dreamer has the choice of changing the structure completely, perhaps using the rubble that is left, or of maintaining the external structure and rebuilding and reshaping the internal thoughts and ideas. In many cards of the Tower, there is an image of a crown, suggesting the highest spiritual attainment through tribulation. Whatever happens, the card represents radical change.

In the present dream, it is this spiritual attainment that is highlighted, though the towers are not struck by lightning but by the planes – practical attempts at freedom of movement. Understanding how she has constructed her life in ways that have worked for her up until now, the dreamer is being shown in the image of the smaller tower that conflict and difficulty can stifle initiative. The larger tower, and the fact that she is flying by her own efforts, shows her that with a return to previously held beliefs, she could attain greater freedom.

CHARACTERS AND PARTICIPANTS

The beings involved in your dream may be people, animals, birds or other creatures; they may even be supernatural beings, mythological men or beasts. We may recognize them as belonging to our everyday world if they are friends, family, work colleagues or familiar pets. Alternatively, they can be a bizarre intruder in our dream – a bull in a china shop. They can provide not only symbolic associations but also perspective, as we can sometimes also look at the dream from that character's viewpoint.

PEOPLE

When a person appears in a dream scenario, he or she is a little like an actor in a play, being there to convey an idea or a concept.

THE IMAGERY

It is thought that almost every character who appears in our dreams ultimately reflects a part of our own personality. Such characters can often be better understood if, during interpretation, we put ourselves in the position of that person. Rather than asking the character what it is doing in your dream, it can be illuminating to shift perspective and consider the dream from the character's point of view. That way we may also be able to clarify our relationship structure, which is looked at in more detail in the section on Emotions, Reactions and Responses (beginning on page 181).

Dreaming of ourselves as an *adolescent* suggests that we concentrate on the undeveloped, perhaps immature, side of our personality. We might ask ourselves then whether we need to support that part, give it expression in waking life, or allow it to mature by using the techniques of creative visualization and meditation. Such a figure will very often be a representation of the Fool in the Tarot as he sets out on his journey.

An adolescent of the opposite sex often means we need to deal with a suppressed part of our development. There may be conflict over freedoms both given and taken by others and, depending on gender, could be dealt with more sensitively or more logically.

Our impression of authority is usually first developed through our relationship with our father or father-figure. If we have had a domineering father, a known *dictator* may appear in dreams as representing that relationship. If in addition we have difficulty with authority figures in general in waking life, a personification of dictatorship may appear in dreams.

Often, depending on how we were treated as children, our view of authority will be that it is anything from a benign helper to an exploitative disciplinarian. Most authority figures in dreams will ultimately lead us back to what is right for us, although not necessarily what we might consider good; our wilder, more renegade side needs controlling. A *king* emerging in a dream usually represents the father or father-figure and our need for approval.

When the king is *old or on the point of dying* we will be able to discard old-fashioned family values that may be hindering us. A *new king* might suggest a new or different form of authority, such as a new boss, in our waking lives. An *emperor or foreign ruler* appearing in our dream may indicate that some of the father's attitudes and ways of being may be alien or indeed literally foreign to us.

The figure of a *queen* in dreams often represents our relationship with our mother, and thus with women in authority generally. Since the queen represents ultimate authority or approval, we may dream not only of any present queen, but also a *historical*

one such as Victoria or even a *fantasy or mythical* one. We have seen some of the interpretations of both sorts of royalty figures in the interpretations of the court cards in the Minor Arcana in the Tarot.

To dream about a *baby*, particularly *one that we feel to be ours*, highlights those vulnerable feelings over which we have no control. We may also be considering a new project or way of life that is literally 'our baby'. Dreaming of *a foetus* rather than a live baby suggests that a project or idea has not yet been properly formed sufficiently for it to survive on its own. If the *baby is someone else's* in the dream we need to recognize that a situation in waking life is not our responsibility or that we should not interfere.

Dreaming of a *child* gives us access to the less-developed sides of our personality – the inner child at a specific stage of development. We all have parts of ourselves that are still child-like and inquisitive. Dreaming of *our own children* highlights the special dynamic inherent in family relationships.

A dream about a *boy* shows the potential for development through new experiences and being in touch with ourselves at a young age and with the unsophisticated naivety and passion that a boy has. We are connecting with our natural drives and ability to face difficulties. When a *girl* of any age appears in our dreams we are usually attempting to make contact with the more sensitive, innocent, intuitive,

feminine side of ourselves. If the girl is *known to us* we probably are aware of those qualities, but need to explore them more fully. If she is *unknown*, we can acknowledge that a fresh approach from a different perspective would be useful.

In dreams, the *elderly* very often represent either our forebears or ancestors and hence wisdom accrued from experience. Our conformity, ways of behaving and ethics are largely handed down from generation to generation. *People older than us*, who are not necessarily elderly, usually signify our parents or some form of parental control. *Groups of elderly people* frequently appear in dreams and signify the traditions and wisdom of the past – those things which are sacred to the 'tribe' or family.

THE SIGNIFICANCE

The ultimate goal in understanding ourselves and living a successful life is what psychoanalyst Carl Jung called individuation. This is a growth towards maturity and an acceptance that all parts of our being can work together in harmony. When we learn to use them all as successfully as we can, we consciously begin to integrate those parts of our personality as we undertake our journey.

There is a particular group of behaviour patterns within each of us as an individual that makes us uniquely recognizable. In dreams these patterns and characteristics can be magnified so that they are easily identifiable –

they can often appear as separate personalities or characters. Much energy and power can become available once their significance is understood.

Our interaction with people in ordinary life and with our dream characters has the effect of highlighting that growth. When we are no longer afraid of any aspects of our personality, we do not project them on other people, nor do we permit other people to use us as 'punchbags' by pressing our particular triggers. Thus, an *individual from the past* could link us with a particular period in our lives, or with certain memories that may, or may not, be painful.

A particular person's appearance in a dream may be significant because of the very ordinariness of the occasion, or alternatively because their behaviour is bizarre. This may be because the dreaming self wishes to highlight a

particular aspect of either our character or actions in waking life. Dream characters may emphasize aspects of their occupation or indeed may even offer explanations of our past actions. Only you as the dreamer will, with practice, be able to understand the significance to you.

Any *masculine figure* that appears in a dream demonstrates an aspect or facet of our essential being, usually our drives or the more logical side of our personality. Such a figure can identify the Shadow (the negative side of himself) for a man, and the Animus or hidden masculine for a woman. *A man in a woman's dream* suggests that she is becoming aware that she has, or can develop, all the aspects of the masculine that enable her to reach her full potential. If the man is *one she knows* or loves she may be trying to understand her relationship with him. An *unknown*

man or stranger is generally that part of our personality that is not yet recognized. *A well-built or large man* appearing in our dreams indicates either our appreciation of the strengths, certainties and protection which our basic beliefs give us, or suggests that we may be feeling threatened or are made apprehensive by those very qualities. When we become aware of cultural characteristics in a male figure in dreams, we may be touching into our own understanding of stereotypes or the somewhat unconventional side of ourselves.

Any *woman* appearing in a dream represents all the qualities that we understand as feminine. Such a figure in dreams can suggest the softer, more intuitive aspects of the personality. In *a man's dream* such a figure describes his relationship with his own feelings and perhaps how he relates to his female

partner. In *a woman's dream* a female family member or friend in particular is often representative of an aspect of her own nature, but one she has not yet fully integrated. More spiritually, a *goddess or holy woman* signifies the highest aspect of the feminine that can be attained. It usually suggests intuitive wisdom and the need to work for the greater good. *An Oriental woman* appearing in a dream is taken to suggest the enigmatic, mysterious side of the feminine. The Oriental way of life appears to be more gentle and perhaps more intuitive than the Western. In dreams we tend to link with the side of ourselves that can access wisdom and clarity. This tends to be a feminine way of working.

An *older woman* most often represents our mother and her sense of inherited awareness and wisdom as epitomized by the crone or wise woman. An *unknown woman* in dreams will represent either the Anima (his sensitive side) in a man's dream, or the Shadow in a woman's. We can actually gain a great deal of information because the figure is unknown, and therefore needs to be carefully considered. It is the element of surprise and intrigue that permits us to explore the relevance of that previously hidden figure further. She is epitomized by the High Priestess in the Tarot.

SUBSIDIARY IMAGES AND ASSOCIATIONS

It is often difficult to decide the exact relevance to us of the people who appear in our dreams. Sometimes it is our relationship that is important, sometimes it is what they represent, and sometimes they are simply there to highlight a particular aspect of the dream. Family (which we consider shortly) and *friends* can therefore be difficult to categorize. We need to look at our relationship in waking life with that particular person in order to work out whether that relationship is negative or positive. Then we need to decide what they represent for us – for instance security, support and love.

Just as in the Fool's Journey each character allowed us to learn a little more about ourselves, so each dream character does the same. As an example, in dreams, when we become aware of a burglar or intruder, a part of our psyche may have previously been neglected, and is now intruding on our awareness. A *burglar* will want something we already own. With an *intruder*, it may be that there is some form of violation of our private space in waking life; we are feeling threatened in some way. Often in dreams the intruder or burglar is masculine, and this generally indicates a need to defend ourselves in some way. If the intruder is feminine it may highlight an element of seduction or undue persuasion in everyday life. When the figure is identified as a *thief*, we become aware of part of our personality that can waste our own time and energy on meaningless activity. The thief in the spiritual sense is the trickster, the villain, who 'steals' our respect for self.

An *outlaw* signifies someone who has gone against the laws of society. To dream of a *decrepit old wanderer or tramp* links us back to the part of ourselves that may not be expressed fully in real life. It is the 'drop-out' within us. We may be becoming conscious of our need or desire for irresponsibility. Incidentally, although this image starts out as negative, if we are prepared to work with it, it can have great positivity since ultimately the character is always in the right place at the right time for the right reasons, and often matures into the *Hermit*, who we have met already in the Tarot.

There is one group of people about whom most of us will dream at one time or another. Part of the human personality both needs – and yet abhors – adoration, so such figures as *celebrities, media personalities and sports stars* appearing in our dreams allow us to work out this dichotomy. It may be that we ourselves seek similar adoration. We are attempting to identify what qualities these people have that we feel are lacking in us. Celebrities can personify 'the chosen ones', those from whom we expect a certain standard of behaviour, and on whom we can project our disapproval. To be in an audience – perhaps watching such personalities – tends to highlight the multiple parts of our own personality and it may be that we are witnessing an emotion or process of change in ourselves. To be *seeking an audience*, perhaps with a religious figure, denotes an approach to Divine power.

Dreaming of being *in a crowd* of any sort could also be indicative of the fact that we do not wish to stand out, or that we do not have a sense of direction at present. We want to retain our anonymity, to create a façade for ourselves or, conversely, to join a group of like-minded people – to belong. The purpose of a group appearing in dreams may be to draw our attention to the validity of group thought – that we can relate to people who think and feel the same way as we do.

Any *group of people or grouping of articles* in dreams actually highlights the energy and power that that grouping creates. It is greater than the sum of its parts. If we find ourselves on the *outside of a group* then we must find common ground. For instance, when a jury appears in a dream we are usually struggling with an issue of peer pressure. We may fear that others will not understand our actions, that they could judge us and find us wanting.

A *mob or gang*, with its slightly more negative connotations, represents group energy that has become uncontrolled or unrestrained. It can appear quite threatening and may mirror a situation in waking life. For a man to dream that he is in a harem or group of women shows that he is struggling to come to terms with the complexities of the feminine nature. For a woman to have the same dream shows that she is beginning to understand her own flamboyant and sensual nature, and perhaps relishing the idea of belonging to a group of supportive women.

PREGNANT GIRL DREAM
This example shows how a specific dream can be interpreted.

THE DREAM
'A pregnant girl visits me with her mother who is holding a black plastic bucket. Inside the bucket is an embryo submerged in a special distilled fluid. The girl has to wait until the embryo is fertile before she can put it inside of her. She has lost one before so she is taking extra care with this one. They come to visit me to show me the embryo.'

THE INTERPRETATION
First, it is important that the dreamer realizes that the embryo is not a real baby, but in dream interpretation symbolizes a new beginning, a new project, or even a new way of thinking about herself. A bucket, as a hollow container, almost always represents femininity and as black plastic is not 'natural' – it is a somewhat manufactured concept of femininity. You have two examples of the feminine here, the mother and the daughter. The embryo has not yet quite become real, and must become more so, for the girl in the dream, before she can accept it and place it within. Nevertheless, she is already recognizing the potential, since she is seen as being pregnant. The girl – the part of you that is nurturing and caring – recognizes how special this new concept is as the fluid (emotions surrounding this) is specially distilled. She also understands that she has got things wrong before so must be extra careful. The relationship with the mother either represents the dreamer's own relationship with her mother, which is very special, or her relationship with the Great Mother and the idea of total femininity.

Here we have a slightly negative aspect of the High Priestess Tarot card as someone who is ready to grow in awareness and knowledge, but not yet ready to take on full responsibility for her own fruitfulness.

FAMILY

Images of our family and people we know appear frequently in dreams. Recent studies have discovered that women tend to dream of family 15 per cent of the time and men 9 per cent.

THE IMAGERY

Those considered to be close family are representative not just as themselves but also of aspects of the dreamer's personality (see information panel). The *father or father-figure* thus represents the masculine principle and that of authority, law and order while the *mother or mother-figure* signifies the nurturing, protective principle. In a man's waking life the father tends to become a role model for his behaviour and how he lives his life. In a woman's life the father is the blueprint on whom she bases all later relationships with the masculine.

Other members of the *extended family* can also represent specific concepts and ideas. For instance, *grandparents* appearing in dreams denote not only our attitude to them as people, but also to the traditions, beliefs and inherited characteristics handed down by them; they can often represent old-fashioned values. *Grandchildren* appearing may be an aspect of life affirmation, a passing on of traditions or a promise of better things to come.

THE SIGNIFICANCE

Images of the family, being the first people we relate to, have a great deal of significance in dreams. The family structure is the first secure image that a child latches on to. We know, for instance, that generally a man's first close relationship with a woman is with his mother or mother-figure; similarly, a woman's first relationship with the masculine is usually with her father or father-figure.

All our future relationships, both intimate and platonic, are influenced to some degree by the ones we first develop within the family. Thus our position within the family will also influence our perceptions. Sometimes, through circumstances not within our control, such as illness, death or separation, those relationships can become distorted. Later dreams will either attempt to confirm the distortion or, as we reach a mature understanding, put this image right.

Almost all of the problems we come across in life are mirrored within the family, so in times of stress we will often dream of previous problems or scenarios that have been experienced, or our dream will remind us of that familial situation. When such dreams happen on a fairly regular basis it is perhaps time to address the initial difficulty. It is as though a pattern is laid down which, until it is consciously challenged, will continue to appear. *Rivalry between* siblings, for instance – a common problem in life and in dreams – can usually be revealed as a feeling of insecurity and doubt, possibly relating to whether we feel we are loved enough within the family set-up.

The antagonistic patterns of behaviour between family members are fairly distinctive, and it is often easier to work these through in dreams rather than in waking life. Very early on in life a child moves through extreme self-involvement and interest to an almost exclusive relationship – usually with the mother.

Next comes a different relationship with the father or father-figure who clearly has an existing relationship with the mother, sometimes being perceived as a threat. Therefore, we may dream of *arguing with a family member*, but the significance depends both on other aspects of the dream and also our everyday relationship with that person.

SUBSIDIARY IMAGES AND ASSOCIATIONS

Learning how to love outside the family is a necessary sign of maturity. To dream of a *conflict* between a loved one and a member of our family,

SIGNIFICANCE OF FAMILY MEMBERS

Family members in a dream represent aspects of the dreamer's personality.

FAMILY MEMBER	SIGNIFICANCE
Father or father-figure	Largely an authority figure, whether benign or otherwise
Mother or mother-figure	Nurturing and caring, although may be destructive
Parents	Initial relationship template, possible role reversal as parents age
Husband	A woman's inner masculine traits, drive etc.
Wife	A man's inner feminine traits, sensitivity etc.
Brother	Similarity or rivalry
Older	Experience and authority
Younger	Vulnerability or rivalry
Sister	Sensitivity and similarity
Older	Capability and caring
Younger	Sibling rivalry or inappropriate behaviour
Son	The need for self-expression, parental responsibility
In a father's dream	Unfulfilled hopes, dreams and desires
In a mother's dream	Her own ambitions, sense of continuity and perhaps disappointments
Daughter	Supportive relationship
In a father's dream	Fears of vulnerability
In a mother's dream	Potential rivalry and/or friendship

though there is no overt animosity shown, reveals that we have not really differentiated between our needs and desires for each person. The idea of a *family member intruding* in dreams or actually interfering signifies that family loyalties may obstruct our handling of a particular relationship.

The fairly common dream of a *man's mother being transformed into another woman* signifies a profound conscious change in him. This transformation suggests some deepening of his understanding of women and, depending on the particulars of the dream, such a change can be either positive or negative. It is often a sign of growth and maturity, enabling him to realize that he can move away from the need to be mothered.

Equally, in dreams where a *woman's father, brother or even lover turns into someone else* she needs to become more independent. If she has not already consciously recognized the need as a teenager, a woman must learn to 'walk away from' or adjust her relationship with her father or father-figure, moving towards more rounded relationships.

When a *man dreams of his father* he may be ready for a more fulfilling life if the relationship has been a good one in childhood. If the relationship has been difficult it may be time for him to readjust his perception of his father in some way. For instance, if we dream that our *parents are somehow suffocating us* and thus forcing us to rebel, then we need to break away from childhood behaviour and develop

more fully as an individual. Dreaming of a *parent's death* can also have the same symbolism.

In dreams as an adult we are able to control family images in order to work through our difficulties without harming anyone else, perhaps using dream management techniques. It is worth mentioning that one person working on their own dreams can have a profound effect on the interactions and unconscious bonding between other members of the family in waking life.

Dreaming of our *partner or spouse*, depending on the content of the dream, often highlights our own feelings of validity within the relationship. It is about how we express our own gender. Within each of us is the recognition of our own drives and sensitivity, some of which may be hidden or suppressed. Partnering of any sort is frequently a search for that compatibility which allows us a safe space to express the hidden part of ourselves. An opposite gender partnering, as with a *same-sex partnering*, allows us to express the various aspects of our personality that may well not be appropriate in other circumstances.

To dream of our partner therefore gives access to awareness and information that reflect our own self-approval and commitment. Dreaming of *having a partner when we do not have one in waking life* suggests that we have partially succeeded in integrating within ourselves the overt qualities of the dream partner. Dreaming of *not having a partner* may be a search for

emotional freedom or from responsibility. Dreaming of the *death of a partner or spouse* can suggest that we have lost touch with an important part of our own make-up – the inner masculine or feminine which provides us with a sense of balance and integration. Such a dream is often followed by one that demonstrates how we can recover that lost part or achieve a different perspective of ourselves.

Dreaming of having a *son or daughter when we don't have one in waking life* is an extension of the idea that dreaming of a baby is a new project. A son may represent the urge to create something of value; a daughter would suggest a more disparate, creative urge – one that has not yet been given form or manifested. Members of the *extended family* (aunts, uncles, cousins, nieces and nephews and so on), apart from appearing as themselves, will often highlight certain character traits within ourselves, or shared family values.

A relationship that seems to be *incestuous in a dream* may signify that the dreamer has become fixated in some way on the relative's behaviour, needing to integrate an aspect of the other's personality with their own. Family members suffering from *injury*, or appearing to be distorted in some way, reflect our fear for or about that person.

ANIMALS

Animals appear frequently in dreams and usually represent aspects of our personality that can be most easily understood on an instinctive level.

THE IMAGERY

By returning to, and understanding, instinctive behaviour we are able to realign ourselves with our own inherent life force. This imagery and symbolism in dreams can be easily perceived once we realize that there is a degree of anthropomorphism involved; we invest our animals with very human qualities – the lion being considered regal, for instance. In this Imagery section we have included some familiar animals that tend to appear in dreams. These include domesticated and farmyard animals as well as some wild animals. By understanding animals and their symbolism, we are able to approach life in a simpler and more natural fashion.

Because shamanic societies were so close to their animal counterparts it was simple to adopt them as guides and mentors and friendly totems, and included here is a necessarily brief table of animals that have both totemic and cultural symbolic significance (see information panel).

Some animal images will have negative interpretations and some positive. Equally, what the animal is doing will influence whether or not there is a positive meaning to the image.

Popular belief has it that *bats* are frightening and dreaming of them attacking us shows the need to confront our fears and phobias; a *flying bat* can represent discernment or obscurity of a spiritual kind. The *camel* represents wise use of available resources and obedience to the basic principle of survival. It also symbolizes the qualities of stamina and self-sufficiency.

The *cat* often denotes the capricious side of the feminine. The refined but also the powerful yet self-reliant aspect of woman may also be suggested. Bast, the Egyptian cat goddess, has both a destructive and protective side to her nature.

When a *dog* appears in dreams it will often have the same symbolism as that seen in the Fool card in the Tarot. We may need to recognize either a devoted and loyal companion or a protector. To dream of a *pack of wild dogs* portrays emotions and feelings of which we are afraid. A dog *guarding gates or*

TOTEM ANIMALS

A totem is a natural object or animal that has personal symbolic meaning, and with whose energy we feel an affinity. Today, as we rediscover the simplicity of this connection, we too can create those links; such animals will make their appearance initially in dreams.

ANIMAL	TOTEM MEANING	SYMBOLISM
Bear	Power of the unconscious	All-caring mother
Bull	Fertility, relationship	Sexual passion, creative power
Cow	Nurturing	Eternal feminine, power of the group/family
Deer	Gentleness, innocence	Pride, nobility, status
Donkey/Ass	Wisdom, humility	Patience, obstinacy, determination
Fish	Knowledge, determination	Worldly and spiritual power
Fox	Shapeshifting, invisibility	Crafty behaviour, cunning
Giraffe	Farsightedness	Expression, communication
Goat	Surefootedness, reaching fresh ground	Creative energy, masculine vigour
Hare	Leaps of faith	Intuition, spiritual insight
Hedgehog/Porcupine	Defence against negativity	Tenacity, strength of purpose
Jackal/Coyote	Wisdom, folly	Transformation of negative energy into positive
Jaguar	Courage	Balance of power
Kangaroo	Responsibility	Motherhood, protection, strength
Lamb	New life, sacrifice	Innocence
Lemming	Valour, use of available resources	Balance, introspection
Leopard	Invisibility	Stealth, hardiness
Lion	Leadership, honour	Dignity, strength, courage
Lynx	Inner secrets, hidden knowledge	Objectivity, clarity of vision
Monkey	Communication	Inquisitiveness, mischief
Moose	Awareness, sensitivity	Power, energy
Elk	Strength, nobility	Stamina
Mouse	Attention to detail	Shyness, reticence
Otter	Playfulness, joy	Resilience, sensitivity
Ox/Buffalo	Right action	Hard work, untiring
Puma/Cougar	Responsibility, empowerment	Grace, strength
Rabbit	Family, mothering	Fertility, sensuality
Ram	New beginnings	Energy, authority
Sheep	Purity	Group support
Squirrel	Preparation, activity	Hoarding, guardianship
Tiger	Passion, devotion	Dignity, power
Wolf	Guardianship, hierarchy	Teaching, free will

being near a cemetery symbolizes the guardian of the underworld. In Egyptian mythology this is depicted by Anubis, the dog-headed god.

An *elephant* appearing in dreams signifies loyalty, memory, patience and strength. The elephant is also a symbol of Ganesh, the Hindu god of opportunity.

Fish generally signify both temporal (worldly) and spiritual power. Dreaming of fish connects not only with our emotional side but also our ability to be wise without being strategic, to go with the flow. To be dreaming of *fishing* suggests we are searching for information.

The *hedgehog* can represent wrongdoing and rudeness or, quite literally, our inability to handle a 'prickly' situation.

The figure of a *horse* in dreams represents our intrinsic vitality. Traditionally, a *white horse* describes our state of spiritual awareness whereas a *brown* one represents our more rational and sensible side; a *black* horse is our excitable side. A *pale* horse suggests Death, and a *winged horse* depicts the soul's ability to transcend the earthly plane. If the horse is *under strain or dying* we may be having problems with motivation. *Riding* a horse suggests that we have 'harnessed' those drives and motivations which carry us into the future. *Falling off* a horse suggests we have not yet controlled the energy inherent in our more powerful side.

Because of its scavenging nature, the *hyena* is taken in dreams to signify imperfection, lack of stability and deviousness. It can represent the darker side of human nature, but equally signifies the Transformer of bad into good.

The *kangaroo* often stands for motherhood, protection and also strength.

In its more negative connotation, the *leopard* represents oppression and aggression and, traditionally, the underhandedness of power wrongly used. If it is the spots that are noticeable, there may be a situation in our lives that cannot be changed.

The *lion* can represent the developing ego and the associated feelings and emotions. It is perceived at its most powerful in the Strength card in the Tarot. A *lion lying with a lamb* suggests that there is a union, or compatibility of opposites – instinct and spirit going hand in hand.

The *mole* is often taken to represent the powers of darkness, but can signify the heedless perseverance and tenacity that enables us to succeed. We move short-sightedly forward, ignoring any undermining influences.

A dream of a *mouse* shows there may, quite literally, be an aspect of chaos 'gnawing' at us in waking life.

The *pig* suggests a kind of earthy sensuality and *big litters of piglets* can represent fertility. Since the *sow* can also depict the archetype of the Destructive Mother, that fruitfulness can, however, be somewhat tainted. The pig traditionally indicates

the lower qualities of ignorance, selfishness and greed. However, without recognition of these qualities we cannot attempt to master or transmute them.

A *white rabbit* may show us the way to the inner spiritual world and, as such, act as a guide on our journey.

The *ram* signifies the qualities of leadership necessary within a flock or group and therefore can represent the dedication needed for such a task. The *sheep* is renowned for its flock instinct, and it is this meaning – the need to belong to a group – that is most usually accepted in dreams. To dream of sheep and wolves, or of sheep and goats is to register the conflict between good and evil.

In the sense that they are unwanted and invade others' space, any *vermin* represents a negativity that needs to be got rid of. The *rat* in particular can represent something that is repellent or gnawing away at us in some way. Slightly more positively, in some Chinese belief systems the rat represents prosperity and can therefore also represent good fortune.

Weasels, stoats and ferrets, because of their sinuous body shape, all tend to represent a somewhat 'slippery' character. The weasel traditionally highlights the devious, more immoral side of our selves. The stoat, while being of the same family, has a different connotation in that in winter it becomes the ermine – a symbol of royalty. In dreams it can, therefore, represent a transformative energy. The ferret, being something of a burrowing animal, can have the same significance

as the mole or that of digging out necessary facts.

The *zebra* has the same significance as the horse, but with the additional meaning of balancing the negative and the positive in a very dynamic way.

THE SIGNIFICANCE

Animals tend to surface in dreams as messengers from the unconscious. It is interesting to note that, from a cultural perspective, it is those animals with which we are most familiar that will tend to appear in dreams. The buffalo/bison is a case in point, having slightly different significance to the Native Americans than it does to the Hindu people of the Indian subcontinent. The former regard the rare white buffalo as sacred, whereas the latter regard all buffalo as sacred animals.

Looked at from a cognitive perspective, such dreams are ways of getting to know parts of ourselves that we have hitherto rejected or not understood. It was not until the 20th century, when psychoanalysts began to explore dreams more fully, that the connection with the cognitive mind was made. Nowadays it is easy to see why our own Dream Oracle will manifest an animal image to alert us to some aspect of ourselves that we need to integrate more fully into our personality.

SUBSIDIARY IMAGES AND ASSOCIATIONS

Our interaction with animals in everyday life is so noticeable that when they occur in dreams, they should be very carefully assessed.

Thus, to dream of trying to *find some refuge* from animals, whether by building defences or perhaps by running away, raises the question as to what action is appropriate in everyday life to protect ourselves from others' aggressions. Any *threat from animals* highlights our own fears and doubts over our personal instinctive urges or those of others. *Taming or harnessing* an animal shows the efforts we are making to control our instinctual responses and make them productive and useful. *Wild animals* in dreams will often stand for danger or dangerous people.

When worn, the *horns of an animal or its skin* were at one time thought to imbue the wearer with the qualities of the animal. Even today this idea can still occur in dreams and, indeed, can be incorporated into creative visualization and meditation when trying to develop certain attributes of our personality.

God-like, talking, awe-inspiring or wise animals, or those with human characteristics, represent the part of us that has an instinctive wisdom and grasp of circumstances, but which is often not listened to in the hurly-burly of everyday life. These and *composite animals* (perhaps the body of one and the head of another) have the same significance as fabulous beasts, covered in the section on Mythological, Magical and Spiritual Creatures (see page 148).

When a *baby animal* appears in a dream we are likely to be trying to understand the child-like side of our personality, or sometimes children known to us. If a *young animal is hurt* we may perceive a difficulty in becoming mature or facing the problems of life. An *animal with a cub* represents motherly qualities, protective instincts and possibly family life. Interestingly, *prehistoric animals* will represent a hidden fear, or trauma from the past or from childhood, while a pet will show that we are reacting to a natural drive in ourselves to give or receive love.

Through a dream about *deformed animals* we can come to recognize that some of our impulses may be offensive to others. We understand our own wrong thinking or warped perceptions. When a *wounded animal* appears, we ourselves may be suffering either emotional or spiritual wounds or difficulties. *Killing an animal* may illustrate the need to come to terms with the energy derived from our baser instincts. The straightforward transformation of a dreamer or other characters into animals and vice-versa shows the potential for change within any situation.

Two other images that arise in dreams connected with animals are the *zoo*, which suggests that we perhaps need to be more objective in our appraisal than subjective, and the *kennel*, which represents a safe space for the potentially more difficult side of our personality, away from harm.

BIRDS

Birds are, by tradition, powerful symbols and have a place in most cultures as having a strong connection with the Divine.

THE IMAGERY

Birds have had significance to humans ever since we first began to observe their behaviour. They were seen to symbolize certain qualities and powers, many of which have relevance even today.

White and black birds can represent any polarity in our waking lives so, symbolically, as we see below, Noah's action in sending out a black bird and a white bird signified the end of one kind of belief system and the beginning of another. In other imagery in dreams, a *caged bird* can indicate some kind of restraint or entrapment; a *pet bird* can denote some dearly loved principle or ideal that we are unable give up; and a *flock* of birds represents a group purpose or ideal.

A bird's *plumage* is its protection, but it is also its power and strength. In a dream, plumage being drawn to our attention can often stand for a display of power and strength, and may also represent the way we present ourselves to the outside world. When the *wings* are particularly noticeable, attention is being drawn to our need for freedom or to the idea of how protective of ourselves we need to be.

THE SIGNIFICANCE

In dreams, from a mundane perspective, birds usually represent self-reliance and imagination. More esoterically, they have often been invested with magical and mystical powers, hence their appearance in many cultures as guides and mentors. They have also over the years come to represent the soul – both its darker and its more enlightened side.

A bird flying freely represents our aspirations and desires and, *flying high*, the spirit set free and soaring towards the Divine. The *golden-winged bird* has the same significance as fire and therefore indicates our spiritual, more esoteric aspirations. In a man's dream a bird can represent awareness of the anima – his inner feminine. In a woman's dream it is more likely to represent the archetypal self – that part of her being that has brought integration of her intuitive abilities.

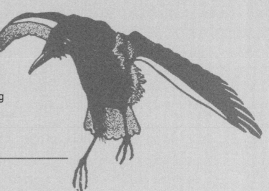

THE SYMBOLISM OF BIRDS

While not exhaustive, this list helps us to gain a little understanding of how the symbology came about, how various qualities were ascribed to the birds and how they have developed as totems over the years. In the modern day, we are fortunate in having access to several schools of thought without necessarily needing to subscribe to one particular culture's symbolism.

BIRD	TOTEM MEANING	SYMBOLISM
Birds of Prey (see also Eagle, Falcon, Hawk)	New vision	Dispassion, superiority
Carrion birds (see also Crow, Raven, Rook)	The magic of creation	Bad luck, death
Cockerel	Sexuality	A new day, vigilance
Chicken/Hen	Fertility	Discretion, mothering
Crow	Prophecy	Trickster
Cuckoo	Intuitive energy	Intrigue, perhaps cunning
Dove	Feminine energy	Tranquillity
Duck	Emotional comfort	Immaturity
Eagle	Illumination of Spirit	Perception
Falcon	Clear judgement	Freedom and victory
Flamingo	Display of talents	Careful watchfulness
Game birds (see also Pheasant, Pigeon, Quail)	Sacred movement	Chosen target, concealment
Goose	Call of the Quest	Everlasting love
Gull	Ritual communication	Freedom, power
Hawk	Development of the psychic	Messenger
Ibis	Magical arts	The soul, perseverance
Jackdaw	Occult knowledge	Treachery, but also good news
Kingfisher	Boldness, opportunity	Honour, peaceful existence
Lark	Transcendence	Joy of creation
Magpie	Intelligence	Treachery, but also good news
Ostrich	Groundedness	Avoidance
Parrot	Mimicry	Gossip, loose talk
Peacock	Spiritual awakening	Understanding, rebirth
Pelican	Unselfishness	Nurturing
Penguin	Lucid dreaming, astral projection	Stability and yet fluidity
Pheasant	Passion and balance	Prosperity
Pigeon	Security of family	Survival against the odds
Quail	Group nurturing	Courage
Raven	Shape-shifting	Wisdom
Rook	The call of magic	Deviousness
Sparrow	Triumph after suffering	Industriousness, productiveness
Stork	Focus	New life and beginnings
Swallow	Objectivity	New beginnings or completion
Swan	Mysticism, mystery	Serenity, divine messenger
Turkey	Shared blessings	Careful planning
Vulture	Purification	Best use of resources
Woodpecker	Rhythm, discrimination	Diligence and hard work

SUBSIDIARY IMAGES AND ASSOCIATIONS

In a much-loved Biblical story, Noah sent first a raven and then a dove to ensure that the Flood was over. The *raven* traditionally was a symbol of the old gods and knowledge and is considered by many to still have this significance today. The *dove* is the bringer of tranquillity after the storm. The *owl* is still perceived as having wisdom and in Ancient Greece was sacred to Athene, goddess of wisdom and strategy. The *crane* in China is also considered to be a wise bird and a messenger of the gods. The *goose* was deemed to be a sacred bird by the Romans, and today reflects the childhood love of stories and myths that we now understand from an adult perspective.

For farmers and fishermen, the flight of birds and the timing of these behaviours would give an accurate forecast as to when seeds should be sown or whether a catch would be good. Much of this folklore has, to all intents and purposes, been lost in an urban society. However, on a very deep level we still resonate with the old ideas and they will surface in dreams, particularly as we study and open ourselves up to these ideas.

When birds appear in dreams it is often helpful to consider their shamanic relevance to discover what subtler, perhaps esoteric, information we are being given. We also can look at the relevance of the symbolism that particular bird has in waking life. We have included a number of birds, with their symbolic dream meaning and their qualities as shamanic totems or guardian spirits, in the information panel on the previous page.

There are many thoughts and ideas about birds that need a degree of freedom to become evident. A *nest* will signify the home or home building. It can represent security within our known environment and the safety of a sacred space. Just before giving birth many women have a nesting instinct that can appear in dreams as an actual nest.

INSECTS AND OTHER CREATURES

We often project our own fears and doubts on to images of things that are not well understood, and this is often the case with dreams involving these groups of animals.

THE IMAGERY

Insects in dreams can represent feelings we would rather do without, maybe guilt or something niggling at our consciences. *Amphibians* and other animals living half on land and half in water, such as *crocodiles*, are often to be feared or placated because they cross the dividing line between the deep and the physical world. The *seal* or the *walrus* can represent our emergence from the instinctive state and can sometimes have the same significance as the mermaid in dreams. To our forefathers, when first discovered, they were almost mythical creatures.

Sharks' skeletons are made of cartilage, not bone, and therefore equally represent a halfway state between creatures from the deep and humans. In dreams, to be *pursued by a shark* can suggest that we have put ourselves in danger and created a difficult situation by entering a predator's territory. Hence in waking life we use the word 'loanshark'. Interestingly, whales and dolphins are mammals that seem to have developed the ability to live in the water, not evolve from it. Symbolically, the *whale* represents the powers of resurrection and the ability to 'come back from the dead' – perhaps revive a moribund project. The *dolphin* characterizes the hidden side of ourselves that needs to be understood and also perhaps the more playful side of our personality.

Invertebrates can also seem somewhat scary and nasty until such time as we begin to understand a little more of their deeper meanings. *Slugs and snails* in dreams, for instance, can represent vulnerability and slowness. To be *moving at*

snail's pace suggests direct planned, careful movement. A *snail shell* is a representation of the spiral (see Numbers, Shapes and Patterns starting on page 106) and the Chinese consider that the *tortoise* carries the pattern of the whole of creation on its back; thus it is a revered figure of wisdom and knowledge. When such images appear in dreams there is usually a subtle message in their appearance. *Crustaceans* such as *crabs and lobsters* will often represent the attempts we make to protect ourselves from emotional trauma.

THE SIGNIFICANCE

In the insect world there is an intelligence that had not been recognized until lately. This is what might be called the 'group mind' where a *swarm or large number* of insects, such as locusts, act together in a very structured manner, usually to ensure survival. This is purely instinctive behaviour and, in dreams, insects often remind us of our own primal instincts. Insects in dreams can also reflect the feeling that something is irritating, 'bugging' or threatening us. They may also indicate our feelings of insignificance and powerlessness.

When there is a need to understand why we do things, we first need to control our basic drives. Many *reptilian* dreams or those about *amphibians* are about control or management of those basic urges. One such example is pictured in the Moon card in the Tarot.

In dreams, the hostile, heartless aspects of our instincts are often portrayed by reptiles and other cold-blooded animals. They are usually recognized as being ultimately destructive and somewhat alien. However, the image of the *snake or serpent* as sustained power is the most potent available, since our most primitive urge is sexual. This idea is also portrayed in Tarot in the Lovers card. Long considered to represent temptation, in fact the serpent in the Garden of Eden might be thought of as the drive to understand the connection with the Divine.

Invertebrates have no backbone and it is this characteristic which becomes most prominent in dreams. Largely because they are incapable of standing upright, they scuttle or move in strange ways. Like monsters in myth they have become representative of the more devious, perhaps evil, side of nature. They can also have a hard shell as protection, an image that is quite symbolic in dreams.

SUBSIDIARY IMAGES AND ASSOCIATIONS

Most creatures that belong to water, particularly to the sea, connect us to what Carl Jung designated the Collective Unconscious – that vast store of imagery that is available to everyone. Dreaming of *swimming with dolphins* suggests putting ourselves in touch with, and appreciating, our own basic nature. Generally perceived by sailors to be saviours and guides, they are considered to have special knowledge and awareness. The *crab*, because of its recognized connection with the Moon, is often perceived as the Great Mother.

Interestingly, the *spider* is also taken to be an aspect of the Great Mother, the weaver of destiny. This is the point at which we recognize the ability to create a perfect pattern, which both nurtures and protects us at the same time. Because the *octopus* also has eight legs, it picks up on this same symbolism. Additionally it can represent the unrestricted movement of the Spirit. It surely cannot be by chance that such eight-legged creatures are perceived in this way. We are reminded here of the significance of the number 8 representing infinity, which is emphasized several times in Tarot.

The *snake or the serpent* has many interpretations in dreams. As a lust for life, which has the potential to degenerate into temptation, it corresponds to the serpent in the Garden of Eden. As the *double-headed snake*, as seen in the symbol for healing known as the Caduceus, it represents good health.

More properly, when that same symbol is seen as spiritual and physical power combined, it represents *kundalini* – the inner power that links humans with the Divine. The image of the *snake with its tail in its mouth*, the ouroboros, is one of the oldest available to humans and signifies completion and the union of the spiritual and physical. This symbol is often seen in dreams

without its full implication being necessarily understood.

The snake's ability to *shed its skin* in dream symbolism is more appropriate as a representation of its transformative powers. This same transformative ability is seen when the *tadpole* matures into the *frog* and perhaps also in the *oyster*, which has the ability to transform an irritant into a pearl.

In dreams, while insects are often also seen as irritants, this is not always so. Bees and beetles are primarily noted for their industriousness. The *bee* can also symbolize immortality, rebirth and order. Folk tales, such as the one about telling one's troubles to the bees, have a basis in truth in that the beehive is said to represent an ordered community and therefore the ability to absorb chaos and negativity. The *beetle*, on the other hand, because of its connection with the scarab, can represent protection from evil. *Parasites* such as *lice*, *fleas* or *bugs* in a dream are a positive warning that we need to be aware that someone is attempting to live off our energy in some way. Fleas are symbolic of the type of distress that is likely to hurt rather than destroy, such as gossip.

Flies alert us to the fact that we have certain negative aspects of our lives that need dealing with, otherwise we are likely to become contaminated.

Maggots can represent such contamination, and the sense of being eaten up by something, of there being an alien idea or concept that can overtake and overcome us. Maggots and *worms* in dreams do usually have some connection with death, but more as a representation of transition and the moving on from mundane concerns.

To dream of *crocodiles, or indeed any reptile*, indicates we are looking at the frightening lower aspects of our nature. We may feel we have no control over these, and it would therefore be very easy to be 'devoured' by them. Our aggressive nature may get the better of us. In ancient Egypt it was thought that Sobek, the crocodile god, had to be worshipped and revered in order to ensure that the Nile river continued to flow.

In agrarian societies insects were given perhaps more significance than we ascribe to them today, and their reappearance in dreams might be considered to be a warning about the management of our resources.

MYTHOLOGICAL, MAGICAL AND SPIRITUAL CHARACTERS

Given the opportunity, images of magical or mythical characters in our dreams allow us to access much forgotten knowledge.

THE IMAGERY

Mythical consciousness is the ability to create stories; magical consciousness is the beginning of the need for power and control. Both are developments of awareness that, pre-dating much of today's understanding, form an integral part of our psyche.

Spiritually, many of us are aware of a greater power. Christian belief, for example, holds to one God, although manifesting in three forms – Father, Son and Holy Ghost. Other religions attribute the powers to various gods and goddesses. As we grow in understanding, we can appreciate the relevance of all such beliefs and rather than being patriarchal this power is seen as an all-pervading energy.

Mythology and the stories that surround the various *gods and goddesses* enable us to make sense of our own need for integration and understanding. When such figures appear in dreams they may appear as vengeful or helpful in turn. It does very much depend on the culture to which we belong as to which particular pantheon will resonate with us. Some people will be more comfortable with the Graeco-Roman gods and goddesses such as Hermes or Mercury, Venus or Aphrodite, whereas others may prefer Eastern figures such as the god Shiva or his consort Parvati. As your own knowledge increases you may also prefer to consider other,

perhaps less well-known, pantheons. The internet is a rich source of information and can be very helpful should you wish to carry out some further research.

As we become more able to access the deeper aspects of our being, figures belonging to myths and fairy stories begin to appear in our dreams and it is often useful to have some idea of what they actually represent. A *knight*, for instance, particularly in a woman's dream, can have the obvious connotation of a romantic liaison – the knight in shining armour. He is also often the guiding principle – that part of ourselves that is sometimes known as the higher self. He symbolizes initiation and a refinement of ideals. As one of the court card figures in the Tarot, in dreams – if we allow him to do so – he will show very clearly the next step we need to take in our quest for perfection.

When in dreams we meet the *wizard, magician, priest, wise old man* or *guru* we are accessing the ancient arts of magic and alchemy. Each such figure symbolizes the knowledge from particular aspects of belief, and usually

with a little thought we can understand the significance of their appearance. The magician might encourage us to explore high – or ceremonial – magic, the priest to explore our connection with the Divine, the wise old man to study philosophy and the guru to look at eastern religions.

When their feminine counterparts appear we would do well to explore the more intuitive aspects of our beliefs. The *priestess*, for instance, might signify the commitment needed in practising the use of true intuition in our dealing with others. The conventional *witch with hat and broomstick*, however, would highlight the use of those powers in a slightly more flamboyant, perhaps less positive way. Achieving a synthesis of these abilities on an inner level would create a great deal of power.

The *enchantress* is such a strong image within both the masculine and feminine psyches that she can appear in dreams in many guises.

As the more negative aspect of the feminine, she can appear as a woman meets her self-destructive side. She is the feminine principle in its binding and destroying aspect; the *evil witch*, and the beautiful *seductress or siren* – woman as temptress. This latter often seems to deceive and distract man from his purpose, yet in his escape from her, he sets himself free. She has the power to create illusion, and the ability to delude others, but ultimately is to be understood rather than feared.

Media treatment of such figures as *vampires* and *werewolves* has increased recently. While this portrayal is perhaps more sympathetic than before, such figures highlight the difficulty in integrating the two sides of our nature: good and evil, animal and human. Consequently they will appear more often in young people's dreams. Fear of the unknown, or of a darker force that appears to be life-threatening, is demonstrated when these creatures appear in dreams.

There are other manifestations of power that become known to us through dreams as we bring about

integration between the spiritual and the emotional self. It is thought, for instance, that dreaming about *giants* means that we are coming to terms with some of the repressed feelings we had about adults when we were children. Any *monster* appearing in a dream represents something that we have made larger than life. We have personalized it so that whatever is worrying us appears as a creature.

Given the freedom to create, the mind can produce both the fantastic and the grotesque. In dream imagery, in order to draw our attention to certain qualities, animals may be shown as having characteristics belonging to other creatures. Such *fabulous beasts* are the result of trying to reconcile two polarities, most often the sacred and the profane. The *Minotaur* is, for instance, a representation of the distortion caused when union with the Divine is not understood or properly achieved. The fearsome and terrifying powers of nature are represented in this interpretation; such untamed power must be contained. Archetypally, there are many combinations which are possible and which will give unlimited potential to the creative abilities within us.

The *griffin*, one of the Four Living Creatures as seen in the Wheel of Fortune card in the Tarot, is a combination of an eagle and a lion and has, therefore, come to represent courage and perspicacity. The *unicorn* indicates unconditional love, the single horn signifying perception. Interestingly, it is said that only a virgin (that is, feminine purity) can tame a unicorn. The *dragon* is a complex yet universal symbol. Seen as both frightening but at the same time manageable, as the Guardian of Power, he rules our passions.

To have a *centaur* appear in a dream demonstrates the unification of two distinct opposites – man's animal instinctive nature and his qualities of human virtue and judgement. The *satyr* on the other hand is a masculine spirit of natural power connected with nature at its most raw. He is pictured as a woodland spirit similar to the god Pan and signifies ecstasy in the power and energy of Life.

THE SIGNIFICANCE

There are two ways in which we can verify our own inner certainties, one from an external source and one from an internal. Myths are the external path and magic the internal. Myths, which are cultural stories originally told to explain ideas, concepts and accepted rituals, contain knowledge of correct conduct and spiritual principles. They reinforce those actions and qualities that have, often apparently magically, brought some aspect of success to heroes, supernatural beings and our ancestors, overcoming evil in the process.

Myths and mythology, the collecting of those stories, are thus the external expression and embodiment of teachings that we have and will always require in order to find our own inner truth and innate power. The ancient systems of understanding the Cosmos and the Divine often give rise to much archetypal dream imagery that, even today, seems magical to the uninitiated. Indeed, we have seen in our exploration of the Hero's and the Fool's Journey the template that helps us to explore our own personal mythology.

Magic previously was perceived as being all about controlling external forces and negative manifestations of power. It may indeed still have that significance in dreams. Psychologically, however, when magic or magical elements appear in a dream it is much more to do with our ability to link with our deepest powers. When we are using magic in a dream, we are using our energy to accomplish something without effort or difficulty. We are capable of controlling the situation that we are in, to have things happen for us and to create from our own needs and wants.

As we grow and mature, dreams become the link between our deepest powers and the external world. The images 'speak' to us, often using the rich imagery of mythology and magic to make a point or direct us towards a new way of thinking. We draw on the old to create the new, and thereby learn to live more comfortably within today's world.

Ancient magical teachings instructed that each of the elements – Earth, Fire, Air and Water – has spirits or entities (*magical beings*) that could be summoned to do the will of the magician, witch or wizard. From today's more scientific perspective there is no better explanation than that these entities are constructs of the mind, whether they can be captured and measured or not. Our experiences of the power of such beings is entirely subjective, albeit shaped by myth and fairytale, so they may appear in dreams in many different guises. Their appearance in dreams signifies our connection with those forces within ourselves.

Traditionally *fairies* were 'hidden people' and, because they are representations of elemental forces, were known to be capricious. Through dreams, therefore, as we develop spiritually and such beings appear, we begin to understand that we are capable of controlling and using natural power. *Nymphs* are personifications of feminine universal productivity and are earth spirits that deal with pure energy. Each group of nymphs has their own particular role and guardianship of specific areas, such as forests and lakes, woods and valleys, mountains and grottoes. *Gnomes* are earthy, gnarled figures and are said to inhabit the centre of the Earth and to guard its treasures. *Elves* are somewhat more ethereal, but are also Earth spirits. All such beings allow us to connect with nature in very specific ways.

Fire spirits are known as *salamanders* and are seen to be the strongest of the elemental spirits. Often perceived as sparks or spheres of light, in dreams they are sometimes seen as lizard-like and somewhat transformative. *Sylphs* are air spirits and often bring inspiration, while *undines* are water spirits and along

with *kelpies* become known when we need a particular aspect of emotional awareness. Some would deem *mermaids, mermen* and *sirens* to belong to the fairy realm. They do, however, have equal validity as mythological figures in their own right. They symbolically represent an ability to be deeply emotional and yet also entirely practical.

When fairy-like *dwarves* or *goblins* appear in dreams, they may symbolize the unconscious and undifferentiated force of nature, signifying that we have not allowed the magical part of ourselves to grow properly.

SUBSIDIARY IMAGES AND ASSOCIATIONS

By the time that both mythological and magical figures appear in our dreams, we are accessing some very archetypal images. Children's imaginations are sparked by fairy stories and moral tales, which enable them to cope with an external world they do not understand. As adults, obtaining fresh access to the imagery of those tales enables us to comprehend and quantify our inner being.

When, in everyday life, events get out of proportion we often have to suppress our reactions. In dreams we cannot do this and so our minds create some way of dealing with the problem. Monsters, dragons and other *fearsome figures* allow us to personalize our fears or sense of evil and, in common with the Hero and the Fool, we can battle with and overcome them. Gentler, more

ethereal spirits, fairy godmothers and *wise animals* usually appear as helpers and supernatural assistants, again allowing us to progress towards greater understanding and a more global perspective.

During spiritual development, our perceptions widen from the ordinary everyday to other aspects and dimensions of knowledge that have become available to us. One of these is what is known as the world of spirit. When *spirits* and what appear to be *ghosts* appear in dreams their function may be to help us through various states of transition. By putting ourselves in touch with what is dead and gone we can take appropriate action in the here and now. While we cope with everyday fears, there are many unconscious memories and feelings – some positive and some negative – which can surface unexpectedly, often in dreams.

Such dreams will often give information through the use of symbology. What the mythological or magical being is doing or holding will be of relevance, so any objects may require interpretation. A chalice or sword, for instance, would have an easily interpreted meaning; further information on magical and spiritual objects can be found in the section on Artefacts and Symbolic Objects (see page 196).

THE EMPRESS DREAM

This complex example shows how a dream can be interpreted using recognized methods, dream imagery and Tarot, and demonstrates the richness of the dual interpretation.

THE IMAGERY

'I am approaching a small church or chapel that has, by the side of the door, a directional arrow to another, more well-known church, significant for its symbolism. The arrow is gold on a green background. The first church is grey stone and reminds me of a simple church that was important to me in childhood.

'My two daughters are with me. We enter the church and the elder one is getting very cross with me. She is beginning to shout at me, something she would not normally do. The younger one, my middle child, is maintaining her composure and is slightly withdrawn. I am already uneasy and remain somewhat disturbed throughout the dream. I know I have to take some kind of action, but sense a degree of resistance in myself.'

THE SIGNIFICANCE

The dream at first glance seems to centre around the female members of the family unit. There are some highly tuned emotions in the dream, some out of character, though this is not apparent until the characters are inside the church. The settings are also meaningful. First the group is outside a church, which resonates with childhood for the dreamer, yet is being directed away from it towards a more publicly known one. The colours in the dream – since they are noted particularly – must have meaning and will require careful study.

INTERPRETATION OF THE IMAGES

CHURCHES As an environment for us to consider our system of belief, a church will represent a place of safety or sanctuary. In this case, the first church has reminders of the simpler time of childhood and of the reassurance of that simplicity. The stone suggests the ability to weather or wear well, and is an aspect of permanence. In the dream, the dreamer is being directed to the second

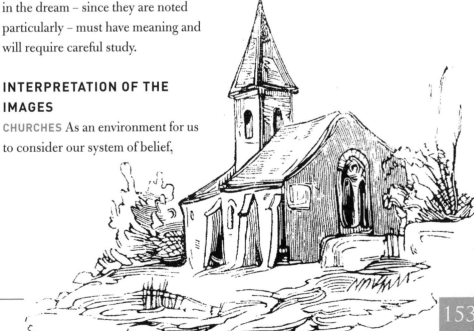

church, which is known to have a more complex set-up and is one where symbolism has to be understood in order to appreciate its beauty. Incidentally, the second church, which has appeared in the media, has a much more public face.

COLOURS The grey of the stone of the church reinforces the idea of a place of permanence and sanctuary. The gold of the arrow suggests emotional security, but also prosperity. The green of the background colour by tradition signifies balance and harmony. Overall, therefore, the colours suggest there is something to be gained by moving from safety to a new way of being.

DIRECTIONAL ARROWS In dreams generally, these suggest a direction that should be taken, the way to go or a particular course of action. The implication here is that there is something to be gained by moving towards a different way of thinking.

PEOPLE People appearing in dreams can have several significances. They may appear as themselves, mirror aspects of our own personality or highlight a particular part of our dream. Our own children can be particularly meaningful.

In this dream, the elder daughter was obviously angry about something, though interestingly the dreamer did not feel in this instance that it was her. The daughter would normally register displeasure by look or by silence, so her behaviour was out of character, suggesting some kind of disquiet. Possibly she was irritated that they had

stopped at the church. Remembering that dream characters can also represent our own feelings, this may reflect the dreamer's own frustration about aspects of her waking life. The dreamer's other daughter tends in waking life to be the peacemaker, and generally accepts the status quo. In this instance, therefore, she is not acting out of character, but reflects the more pragmatic aspect of the dreamer's persona.

It can be seen that there are only female participants in this dream. This leads to the realization that the three aspects of femininity were pictured – maid (unmarried daughter), mother (elder daughter) and the dreamer (crone or wise woman). This is a theme that appears quite frequently in the dreamer's life. The nurturing aspect was uncomfortable in the extreme, and as wise woman she was very much under pressure.

At this stage of interpretation the relevance is not particularly clear. Emotions in dreams can highlight feelings that we perhaps do not allow to surface in everyday life. In this case, both the anger and frustration and the unease need to be consciously dealt with before the dreamer can move on.

CLARIFICATION USING THE TAROT

The feminine aspect is important in this dream, as is the spiritual belief system shown by the churches. Choosing a card from the Major Arcana in order to clarify the meaning of the dream resulted in the Empress

card, which under the circumstances is entirely apt. Depicting the full force of feminine energy, the Empress signifies a need for the dreamer to understand her own inner power in all its facets. She needs to reflect on her actions before being able to move forward. She must also bear in mind her maternal responsibilities.

Interpreting the card has clarified the dream considerably. Passion and anger are very closely aligned in the human psyche, and for this dreamer many changes are about to take place. New experiences will be available, which may change her personal perspective of the world in general.

A move needs to be made from a private appreciation of spirituality to a more public acceptance. This can, however, only be brought about with the co-operation of all parts of her being, particularly the feminine. Resistance to such a move can be dealt with through an understanding of the necessity for such change, especially for the greater good. There is a risk of stagnation, but with the understanding that changes must be made and that the dreamer must be proactive, much can be initiated and accomplished.

Combining the imagery of the Tarot and that of dream interpretation thus gives a much enhanced understanding of the dream and also is of assistance in clarifying thoughts, feelings and courses of action.

INTERACTIONS, QUALITIES AND PRINCIPLES

The characters and symbols in dreams seldom remain static and separate. The reactions and responses of the dreamer impart layers of meaning which, while subtle, are worth recognizing. Not only are interactions between the dreamer and other characters of relevance, but also those between the characters themselves. As well as non-verbal interaction, conversation and communication are also significant. In this section, we also consider the symbolism associated with occupations, including those related to education, and also to images from the sources of our spiritual belief.

BEHAVIOUR, ACTION AND ACTIVITY

In dreams, how we as dreamers and the characters in the dream scenario conduct themselves is pertinent to the overall interpretation of the dream.

THE IMAGERY

Specific actions will usually have specific meaning within a context and should be easily identifiable. Dream characters are part of the dreamer's own play, and here we are only able to suggest certain interpretations for more commonly seen actions.

As an example, a dream character who is *waving* might be trying to attract our attention or to wave goodbye. If we are *being followed* it might indicate that we are leading, being stalked or are forging ahead. *Being kissed* could be in greeting or as a sign of intimacy.

Physical activity in dreams is of particular note. When trying to gain information from what characters do, it is useful to categorize this into activity within a small space or that which entails movement to or from

somewhere else. Thus *washing your hands or getting up from a chair* belongs to the former, while *walking or running* to the latter. If the dream is to yield up all its secrets, we can pick up small details in this way.

In the Wolf Dream (see page 178) our dreamer remarks that she was with a group of Roman soldiers who were *marching*; further clarification would be needed to find out if she herself were marching. She then *changes location* by turning into the field where a little girl is *running ahead, not away* from her. The movement of the wolf towards her initially seems slightly menacing.

Verbal and expressive communication are also relevant within dreams. *Whispering, calling, talking, shouting* and so on will all contain useful information in

interpretation. Variously they show the need for privacy, to attract attention or disapproval. *Silence* when a question is asked, *a grunt, a frown or a shrug of the shoulders* all show varying degrees of disinterest. Within the framework of a dream, our emotions can be very different to those we have in everyday life. They may be more extreme, almost as though we have given ourselves freedom of expression. *A smile or a laugh, applause* or other expression of the connection between characters is always, therefore, worth acknowledging.

Ultimately, although they cannot necessarily be classed as actions, visual clues (seeing, noticing, recognizing etc.), auditory and thinking activities all need to be acknowledged when understanding dreams. There is no actual imagery attached to them, they are simply experienced – there is an interaction that takes place.

THE SIGNIFICANCE

The behaviour we see in dreams, either by ourselves as dreamers or by the dream characters, can be of several sorts. There is what Calvin Hall called 'social interaction', with both friendliness, or what might be called positive interaction, and aggression or negative interaction. Sexuality was a third category, but for our purposes this might be called intimacy.

Our (or others') behaviour in a dream can differ markedly from normal, since the dream state gives us the freedom to highlight aspects

of ourselves of which we would not normally be aware. Occasionally it is therefore easier to ignore any symbology and simply work with the moods, feeling and emotions that have surfaced. Doing this will very often give us a clearer interpretation of our deeper sentiments.

By and large, what the dreamer is doing in a dream usually becomes self-evident and is fairly easily interpreted. What other dream characters are doing, how they are interacting with the dreamer or with one another, equally needs to be assessed. That interaction may be positive in its outcome or negative. Ordinary everyday activities are just as significant as the more unusual; with a little experience in interpretation they can add richness to the meaning. Thus, 'I hurried' is not quite the same as 'I walked quickly', 'I called out to . . .' is not the same as 'I shouted at . . . .'

Movement is also often relevant in dreams, particularly when it involves a change of location through our – or someone else's – activity. It will sometimes clarify our subsequent decisions in everyday life. *Crawling through a hole*, for instance, suggests that we can find a way through a difficulty, but only by adopting an effective way of bypassing the difficulty.

Conversations, or any kind of verbal activity and communication, are also useful for interpreting what is being conveyed by the whole dream. Hearing and listening are an integral part of the interaction between people, so for these

particular activities to be brought to our attention requires us to take careful note of what is going on. *Hearing* suggests registering a sound, speech or noise, whereas *listening* suggests absorbing the actual content of what is being heard.

We are often able to express clearly what we feel and think in dreams, whereas in waking life we may not feel confident enough to do so. The various characters may also express in their deeds or expressions what has not previously been apparent. *Thinking, feeling and assessing* as actual dream activities are also helpful in taking any action forward within the dream. These are usually activities carried out by the dreamer and it may take a little time to get used to recognizing how that applies in the dream.

SUBSIDIARY IMAGES AND ASSOCIATIONS

Activity in dreams is not just movement in the sense of moving from one place to another. Activities and actions can be interpreted in a number of different ways and will obviously change meaning depending on the overall theme of the dream and our own personal associations with that activity. Such activities cannot always be taken in isolation, but can have certain basic meanings.

To be *eating* in a dream shows that we are attempting to satisfy our needs or hunger. Hunger is a basic drive and only once such a drive is met can we move forward to satisfying our more aesthetic needs. A lack of satisfaction may not be acknowledged in the waking state, but can be translated into dream symbolism and become hunger.

Cooking can symbolize creativity of all types, including being prepared to satisfy our basic needs. To *not eat or refuse food* in dreams indicates an avoidance of growth and change and may be an attempt to come to terms with some emotional trauma. *Fasting* is an accepted way of changing consciousness, both in dreams and in waking life. It is also a move towards spiritual realization. *Being eaten by a wild animal* shows the likelihood of us being consumed by our more basic, animal nature.

When facing uncertainty in waking life we very often need reassurance that we have both the courage and the daring to go ahead with a particular activity. To dream of *falling* shows a lack of confidence in our own ability, the need to be grounded. We may feel threatened by a lack of security, whether real or imagined. It could seem as though we are slipping away from a situation – essentially we are losing our place. Very often, to dream of *plunging* is to recognize that we do have the ability to go forward, although that may mean taking a risk.

Floating in a dream was considered by Freud to be connected with sexuality, but it is probably much more to do with the inherent need for freedom and our ability to rise above a situation. To be *flying without assistance* in dreams also suggests a degree of freedom that is not

normally feasible in ordinary life.

Running in dreams does sometimes suggest the potential for anxiety or distress, though today, as many people use it as a form of exercise, it will also depend on our interpretation of the dream environment. Running *in a group*, such as in a marathon, has a very different interpretation to running alone. In a group there will often be a common aim, whereas *alone* we may be trying to attain a personal goal. Dreaming of being alone highlights being single, isolated or lonely. More positively, it also represents the need for independence. Loneliness can be experienced as a negative state, whereas being alone can be very positive.

Repetitive movement of any sort in a dream usually indicates the need to reconsider our actions, to look at what we are doing and perhaps to express ourselves in a different way. *Leaping* suggests bridging a gap, whereas the act of jumping, for instance, can be somewhat ambiguous. Both *jumping on the spot* and *bouncing up and down* can indicate joy and exuberance and have the same significance as dance. Spiritually, *dancing* has always been taken to represent the rhythm of life, so to be dancing in a dream portrays the creation of happiness, feeling at one with our surroundings.

Jumping also has additional meanings. *Jumping up* means we are attempting to attain something better for ourselves. *Jumping down* means going down into the unconscious and those parts of ourselves where we may feel we are in danger. In both the Hero's and Fool's Journeys the search for the hidden aspects of themselves necessitates jumping down into the Underworld.

Such an act requires a degree of focus and to be totally *immersed* – totally focused – on something in a dream indicates we need to be able to concentrate entirely on one particular thought or idea to help us understand ourselves. We need to achieve a kind of stillness that is foreign to most people and therefore initially frightening, while later on it can be a state of peace and tranquillity.

If we are *following someone or something* in a dream we may need a cause or crusade to help give us a sense of identity. We are perhaps more comfortable in a secondary position, rather than out in front. If we are *imitating someone else* in dreams we are conscious of the fact that we possess the ability to be as they are. To be *imitating one's superiors* in particular is to recognize their greater knowledge.

Later on in the book we categorize some specifically positive and negative behaviour in the sections called Positive Interactions and Celebrations (see page 182) and Negative Actions and Interactions (see page 184).

OCCUPATIONS

Just as fairytales and myths give us concepts of times past, modern-day occupations root us firmly in the present.

THE IMAGERY

Rooted in the here and now, occupations in dreams allow us points of contact with creativity and spirituality – the search for Self. As we progress through life, we come to realize that there is a huge store of knowledge that can be worked with to enhance our lives. People appearing in dreams are likely to have a particular significance for us depending on our upbringing and also our own way of working. It would not be unusual, for instance, for nurses and doctors to appear in a therapist's dreams. Below are some occupations and their better-known significances.

Performers and artists of one kind or another may serve in dreams as a projection of the type of person we would like to be. We may, for instance, in real life be shy and withdrawn, but need to be admired and loved. As a stereotype, such figures often represent our creative force and energy that encompasses so much more than simply artistic pursuits.

It is now widely accepted that music itself has a particularly beneficial healing effect. Any *musician* therefore could suggest a healer or therapist, but in today's society they could equally signify celebrity and our wish to be honoured. As we become more aware of the rhythm of life, motifs associated with dance also become more prevalent in dreams. The figure of a *ballerina or dancer* often symbolizes our search for balance and poise, and can also suggest freedom and the joy of movement. An *organist* in dreams, partially through word association with the organs of the body, is a representation of our life force, personal vibration or ch'i, as it is known in the Eastern martial arts.

A *banker* in dreams originally suggested that part of our personality that we entrust with our resources, both emotional and material. Initially an authority figure, he or she may now sometimes be perceived in dreams as the wastrel or the archetypal villain; a great deal will depend on our individual relationship with our own bank in waking life. Dreaming of an *estate or real estate agent*, or indeed

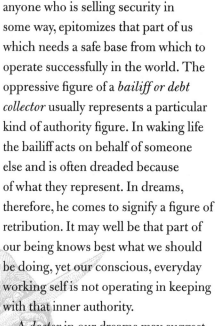

anyone who is selling security in some way, epitomizes that part of us which needs a safe base from which to operate successfully in the world. The oppressive figure of a *bailiff or debt collector* usually represents a particular kind of authority figure. In waking life the bailiff acts on behalf of someone else and is often dreaded because of what they represent. In dreams, therefore, he comes to signify a figure of retribution. It may well be that part of our being knows best what we should be doing, yet our conscious, everyday working self is not operating in keeping with that inner authority.

A *doctor* in our dreams may suggest a known authority figure, and equally someone who has our best interests at heart. Such a figure may also represent a healing energy, in which case a *surgeon* would suggest the cutting out of something negative in our lives. We may in addition be in contact with our own inner *analyst or therapist*. Our instinctive knowledge of what is right for us – our Higher Self – will make itself known in dreams when, on a conscious level, we have diverted from the correct path. Psychologically, the *chemist or pharmacist* represents the part of ourselves which is capable of making changes and is concerned about bodily health. By making calculated adjustments, a situation may be made more positive. An *osteopath* in dreams may suggest that part of us which is capable of manipulating the structure of our lives in order to achieve success, perhaps the release of

trapped energy on any, or all, levels to enable us to reach our full potential. Carers appearing in dreams suggest the more compassionate, nurturing side of ourselves. Often it is that part of the personality which has been 'called' or has a vocation, in which case the dream figure may be that of a nun. *Nurses or carers in the community* may suggest some kind of healing or specific act of palliative care. An *optician*, as someone who cares for the eyes of others, most often represents the need for clarity and wisdom, or rather knowledge specifically applied in our waking lives. It suggests the need to understand a situation that may be confusing us.

Traditionally, when an *alchemist* appears in dreams something 'crude' or basic in our lives may be turned into something worthwhile. Such a figure may also represent ancient or arcane knowledge. Dreaming of an *inventor* connects us with the more creative side of ourselves – someone who is capable of taking an idea and making it tangible. We are also linking with the wiser, if more introverted, side of our personality.

THE SIGNIFICANCE

From the time that we are very small we accept certain stereotypes as having relevance in our lives. Even children's story characters give a sense of the values and requirements of such occupations. As we mature, we give each occupation we encounter certain attributes that will often appear in our dreams.

Dreaming of *being at work* highlights issues, concerns or difficulties we may have within the work situation. When we dream of working at something that does not have a place in our ordinary everyday lives, it may be worth exploring the potential within that line of work or its inherent qualities. We could be actively trying to make changes in our lives, or perhaps having changes forced upon us through unemployment or global recession. Often what we do as a job bears no relation to what we consider to be our real work. Dreams can very often help us to change our situation by giving information as to our real talents and gifts.

SUBSIDIARY IMAGES AND ASSOCIATIONS

Our sense of security – a somewhat intangible asset – without which it is difficult to venture into the world, does need to be properly managed and monitored. The Dream Oracle, with its vast store of stereotypical imagery, can present us with ideas and concepts through the use of occupations. We often have to make our own associations through personal experience. Below are some such figures.

The old-fashioned figure of the *baker* symbolizes nurture and caring, and our ability to change and improve our circumstances by our own abilities. Particularly as television reaches wider audiences, our domestic talents become more discernible and attainable, though

sometimes only by proxy. The *chef* thus symbolizes ultimate skill in a particular art. The *butcher* figure suggests a skilled operator – someone who uses the available resources to the best of their ability and for the greater good. Traditionally, however, he has been

seen as the Grim Reaper or a sign of death. He is of particular service within the community.

Any professional person develops certain talents, such as the ability to do precise work and to 'fashion' something new. The *tailor or dressmaker* signifies

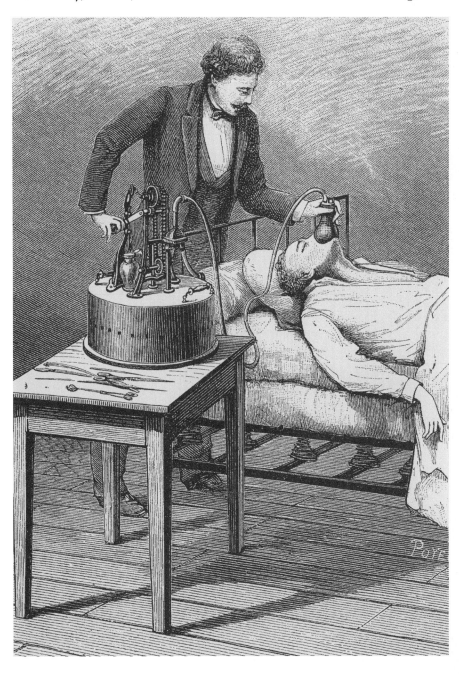

this trained creative energy. As a craftsman, he has worked long and hard to develop these qualities, which are highlighted in dreams.

Often a *fisherman*, like a butcher or baker, will represent a provider, or perhaps bravery, as represented by a *deep-sea fisherman*. A *fresh-water fisherman*, however, may indicate the need for rest and recuperation. Because of the Christian connection with 'fishers of men' a fisherman can also suggest a priest or other religious figure in dreams. In traditional dream interpretation the *hunter or huntsman* represented death. More properly nowadays it is the inevitability of an enforced ending of a situation or some kind of threat specifically targeting us.

The hunter may suggest the provider, though in this time of political correctness he may also represent an outmoded way of behaving. The *gardener* can represent the insights that we have gathered through our experiences in life. They can also represent a specific kind of practical, down-to-earth wisdom on which we can rely. A gardener, as well as a *farmer*, can also signify that part of us which is in touch with the forces of nature, moving with and understanding the rhythm of life.

To dream of an *actor*, particularly a famous one, is to become aware of our own ego and vulnerabilities. Very often we become conscious of the roles we play in life and dreaming of such a character recognizes that we are perhaps not playing the part or behaving as we really want to in life.

In dreams, the *hairdresser or barber* appears as the part of us that deals with self-image, and the way we project ourselves to the world at large. The connection between self-image and beauty is obvious, and we cannot make progress in our lives unless we feel good about ourselves. The interpretation of a dream of waiting at tables depends on whether we ourselves are *waiting at a table*, or whether we are *being waited upon*. If we are in the role of waiter or waitress, we are aware of our ability to care for, and nurture, other people – to be of service. If we are being waited on, we perhaps need to be nurtured and made to feel special.

EDUCATION

When we are relearning how to deal with the growth of our own personalities, the school or classroom will often appear in dreams.

THE IMAGERY

Schools will often appear at times when we are attempting to get rid of old, outmoded ideas and concepts. When we are looking for guidance, it can be presented in dreams as a teacher. Often the figure will be that of a *headmaster*, *headmistress* or *professor* (someone who 'knows better').

A *lesson* is a previously planned form of instruction, the best and most efficient way that we can learn. It will very much have this meaning in dreams, and is truly an application of the Dream Oracle. Dreaming of being in a *university* highlights our own individual potential and learning ability. Since a university is a place of 'higher' learning, we are being made aware of the breadth of experience and increase in knowledge available to us. A *tutorial* implies one-to-one or small group teaching, so in the mundane sense will signify a need for us to understand specific ideas and concepts.

THE SIGNIFICANCE

School is an important part of everyone's life. If we are learning new abilities or skills in waking life, the image of a school will often come up in dreams. It is also the place where we experience associations that do not belong to the family, and can therefore suggest new ways of learning about relationships. We should also be considering our own need for discipline or disciplined action.

For many people, a teacher is the first figure of authority they meet outside the family. That person has a profound effect and the teacher is often dreamt about in later years. From any

perspective, teaching is the passing on of information of things we need to know. Dreams are an efficient way of giving us such information and with practice can be used effectively to help ourselves and others. Those teachings that we receive intuitively and in dreams have the greatest relevance as we progress on our journey.

SUBSIDIARY IMAGES AND ASSOCIATIONS

Dreaming of educational *exams* is most often connected with self-criticism and our need for high achievement. The learning of spiritual concepts is individual to each of us, so the image of a tutorial or other *one-to-one teaching* allows us access to the Higher Self or Inner Guru. It may also show that we should be prepared to share the knowledge and experience we have with others.

The teachings of spiritual leaders and gurus tend to appear to us in dreams in the form of holy books of any kind that are 'required reading'. *Receiving a qualification* in dreams indicates a kind of inner initiation and also the knowledge that we have achieved a goal. We can be rewarded for having reached a degree of competence.

BELIEF SYSTEMS

Our own spiritual or religious background will inform our dream symbolism in this area and create powerful images with a strong grounding in the Collective Unconscious.

THE IMAGERY

Ceremonies and rituals in dreams are highly potent images. They are all part of the heightening of awareness that occurs on the path or journey to spirituality. There are obviously certain ceremonies that are specific to each system of belief. In dream ceremonies the imagery is extremely vivid; because they touch on our own instinctive sense of being they can be very specific. While often based on known rituals they will always have a personal touch.

Dreaming of *religious festivals* such as *Christmas, Diwali, Hannukah, Imbolc* and *Vesak* all signify the beginning of a new phase of existence or a rededication of the Self. Such festivals are usually associated with miracles or the provision of light, signifying a newfound spirituality. Other festivals, which today have become secularized to a large extent, symbolize the gifts of the creator to humanity.

While *archangels* seldom appear spontaneously in dreams without our having consciously linked with them, they are a higher order of angels

and traditionally are considered to be closest to God, particularly in the Judeo-Christian systems of belief. The four best known are Michael, Raphael, Gabriel and Uriel. They may, through creative visualization, be called upon to help us in our understanding. In spiritual terms, the *angel* symbolizes pure being and freedom from earthly matters. As more people become interested in, and seek knowledge about, spirituality there are those who have become more aware of the angel form, particularly in dreams. *Dark angels* are reputed to be those angelic beings who have not yet totally rejected the ego or earthly passions. *Warning angels* usually highlight wrong action.

Appearing in dreams, the *Christ figure or any ancient religious leader such as Buddha*, who taught of the Qualities of Being (loving-kindness, compassion, joy and equanimity), epitomizes the ability to reconcile the physical and the spiritual, God and mankind. The *Christ figure* personifies perfect man. *Appearing on the cross*, he signifies redemption through suffering. Any act of sacrifice in any of in Christian terms, obviously they are also present in all religious figures.

We all are aware of our need for sanctuary from the batterings of the everyday world. Within the *church* or other sacred space such as a *chapel, synagogue* or *temple* we are free to form a relationship with our own personal god. In dreams we may also have the realization that our body is our temple.

In previous times, the figure of the *Devil* was one to be feared and hated. As the wilder, more pagan side of ourselves, the conventional figure with horns and a tail will often appear in dreams. We may be afraid of our own passions, anger and fear. As a personification of the egotistic side of ourselves, and by extension evil, we often need to have an object to confront. In dreams, as in fantasies, the figure of the devil allows us to do this. If we fear our own wrongdoing, that fear can also manifest as the devil.

Demons, fiends and imps tend to be more personally oriented. We see this in the Tarot card of the Devil, where two imps appear to be subservient to the devil himself. To dream of a fiend or devil usually means that we have to come to terms with a part of ourselves that is frightening and unknown.

religion has the same connotation, that of the human being's need to 'sacrifice' himself through passion and through pain. We do not need to be crucified physically to suffer. Both Christ's death on the cross and the death of Buddha, who chose to die after eating a meal offered to him in good faith, are of this kind. The Christ ideal is that part of ourselves which is prepared to take on our portion of the sufferings in the world by working within the world. The *anarchic Christ* is the part of us whose love and lust for life permit us to break through all known barriers. The *Cosmic Christ* is the part that is prepared to take on Cosmic Responsibility – that is, to be connected with the Universal Truth. While these aspects have been spoken

THE SIGNIFICANCE

Dreams have a way of introducing – or rather reintroducing – us to truths which we have long known to exist. Spirituality is taken to be an inner truth that communicates through our Dream

Oracle and religion as that which links us back to Source; it must be the case that religious imagery, or those images associated with our own belief system, partly assist in that function of communication.

When we deny ourselves access to such a store of sacred imagery in waking life, dreams will often react to this lack and try to compensate by jolting us back into an awareness of our inner spirit. It is not until the individual accepts responsibility for their own existence that true spirituality emerges.

If spirituality – the inner truth that we all hold – is neglected, it will simply not go away. In waking life the closest image we have to neglected spirituality is the devil or the more vengeful Indian gods, such as Kali the destroyer. Our own personalized demons can be even more frightening than these.

If we are prepared to accept that each truth will have its own personal slant, and that we must get back to the basic truth, all dreams can be interpreted from a spiritual point of view. This is especially true of sacred imagery and truths associated with our own belief systems. When we widen our perception to include others not well known to us we will find that our store of dream images is vastly enhanced. It is up to us to learn how to interpret these dream images correctly. Most interpretations given here have had to be stated in general terms and are given only as guidelines to enable you to take on true personal responsibility.

SUBSIDIARY IMAGES AND ASSOCIATIONS

There are many images that are common to all systems of belief, often with their own cultural significances. Figures such as *Father Christmas*, *St Nicholas* or the *Green Man* represent munificence and kindliness. They all represent the idea of good times, blessings and largesse, gifts of spirit that allow us to share good fortune.

Blessings may be thought of in terms of a positive energy from beyond us being channelled towards a specific purpose. In dreams they usually signify a prayer of thankfulness.

In dreams, *religious texts, holy books* and, interestingly, large tomes that we cannot always read usually signify that we are ready to receive additional knowledge. Often iconic figures such as *Moses or other revered figures* appear bearing these books, indicating that we are ready to take control of our own destiny. When this figure appears with a *halo or nimbus* it is a representation of innate spirituality.

Whatever our system of belief, *sacred music*, often specifically dedicated to the perception and praise of our God or gods, consists of those vibrations that lift the spirit and enhance our perception of Divinity. In dreams, because our senses are heightened, the effect of those vibrations is magnified.

Because myth has such a hold on the psyche in many people today, we will often find the figures of *gods and goddesses* appearing in our dreams. By and large, they can be taken as personalizations of our best and worst qualities, and much can be learned by working with the various associations given in the section on the meaning of Tarot.

THE BODY

The body offers a great deal of material for interpretation. Its various systems – skeletal, circulatory, muscular – provide rich imagery that is reflected into every life.

THE IMAGERY

Any *limb* can be taken to suggest the fears associated with gender issues and our core values. *Being dismembered* can be taken in its literal sense – we are being torn apart and need to restructure our lives and begin again.

More specifically, *legs* represent our personal means of support. If the *right leg* is highlighted, this suggests movement in a logical sense and may represent moving forward of our own volition, whereas the *left leg* tends to suggest passive movement, perhaps following someone else's lead.

In dreams the *foot* can have several meanings. It can represent the way we make contact with reality, our sense of pragmatism. It can also suggest our ability to ground ourselves and our sense of stability.

Being aware of the *knees* in dreams again highlights the support we are able to give ourselves, this time from an emotional perspective. To be *on our knees* is symbolic of the requirement for prayer and entreaty and perhaps our inability to move forward without help. *Someone else being on their knees* shows a level of emotional commitment, yet at the same time may also represent an act of submission. The *heel* symbolizes that part of ourselves which is strong and supportive but, at the same time, can be vulnerable. *A winged ankle or foot* suggests a need for a different, more efficient form of expression. To be *grinding the heel into the ground* in dreams suggests determination or anger.

Generally *arms* signify our ability to love, or to give and take. Depending on the position of the arms we may also be indicating supplication or showing passionate commitment. The *hands* are two of the most expressive parts of the body and signify power and creativity (see information panel).

When the dream appears to concentrate on the *abdomen*, there is a need for us to focus on our emotions and repressed feelings. We may need to look at how we protect ourselves from other people's negativity in waking life. When we become

SYMBOLISM OF HANDS

Gesture has always been an important part of communication, which is why the hands in dreams convey so much meaning without the need for words.

IMAGE	MEANING
Clenched fist	A threat
Folded hands	A state of rest or deep peace
Hands covering the eyes	Shame, fear or horror
Hands on the head	Thought and care are necessary
Hands placed in someone else's hands	Surrender
Hands raised towards the sky	Adoration or prayer
Left hand	Passivity and receptiveness
Open hand	Justice
Placed together as if in prayer	Defencelessness or supplication
Pointing finger	A way forward
Right hand	Power and energy
Thumb pointing downwards	Adverse energy
Thumb pointing upwards	Power, beneficial energy
Two hands noticeably different	Conflict between belief and feeling
Two people's hands clasped	Union or friendship
Washing of hands (ours or others)	Rejection of guilt or awareness of difficulties
Wringing hands	Grief and distress

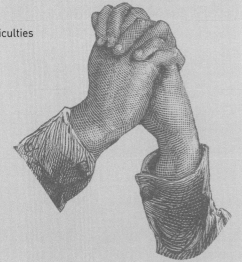

conscious of our own or someone else's *bottom* this may be a play on words in that we have literally 'reached the bottom' of issues. Often in dreams, the mind returns to the initial child-like gaining of the control of bodily functions, particularly that of evacuation. This control is the beginning of self-realization, self-reliance and control, yet at the same time of suppression and defence. Any evacuation of the *bowel* highlights our need to be free of worry; excrement in dreams interestingly enough can highlight financial anxieties. In its more esoteric meaning, it belongs to the realm of feelings. We may simply be trying to get rid of bad feelings that can ultimately be turned into something worthwhile.

THE SIGNIFICANCE

The body forms the prime source of information about us, and often highlights problems we may have. In dreams it signifies the individual and all that he is; additionally it often represents the Ego. Those who appreciate knowledge other than the purely scientific will often find information comes to them through dreams about the body. Psychological stress translated into bodily images often becomes a fertile source of symbolism. When emotions cannot be faced in ordinary everyday life, they very often appear as distorted body images in dreams.

The *head* is the principal part of the body – the motivating force. As the seat of intellect, it denotes power and wisdom. Dreaming of the head suggests that we should consider very carefully how we handle both intelligence and foolishness. To dream of the *head being bowed* suggests prayer, invocation or supplication. When the *head is covered* it shows we may be hiding our own intelligence or perhaps acknowledging somebody else's superiority. A *blow to the head* in a dream indicates that we should reconsider our actions in waking life.

The *hair* represents strength and virility. To be *having our hair cut* suggests that we are trying to create order in our lives. In dreams, to be *combing or brushing* the hair, either our own or someone else's, is to be attempting to untangle a

particular attitude prevalent in our lives. To be *cutting someone else's hair* suggests that we may be curtailing a particular activity. To be *bald* in a dream rather than in waking life shows we are recognizing our own innate intelligence or wisdom.

Any dream where the *eye* is noticeable is connected with our powers of observation and the ability to be discriminating. The eye is connected with the power of light and, in ancient times, to the Sun gods, when it often became a talisman representing perception. *Loss of eyesight* in dreams suggests loss of clarity in waking life; the loss of logic (right eye) or loss of intuition (left eye). *Regaining the eyesight* can indicate a return to innocence and clear-sightedness.

Representing our need to express ourselves, the *mouth* in dreams will often help us to decide how best to handle a situation in waking life. If the mouth appears to be *shouting*, forceful action is required; if *whispering*, a more gentle approach is needed. Dreams of *teeth* are perhaps one of the commonest universal dreams. In old-style interpretation, they were thought to stand for aggressive sexuality, though it is perhaps more appropriate to recognize that, as the teeth are the first visible change in a baby, they represent transition periods in our lives. Teeth falling or coming out easily in dreams mean such a transition is on the horizon.

The *jaw* depicts our way of expressing ourselves. *Pain in the jaw* in dreams can signify our need to release some kind of tension in our lives, possibly by expressing ourselves more fully. Spiritually, the jaw is also thought to signify the opening to the underworld. When we become aware of the *throat* in dreams, we are conscious of the need for self-expression and perhaps of our own vulnerability. The *tongue* is associated with our understanding of information that we wish to pass on to other people; a *forked tongue* can suggest duplicity. The *nose* in dreams can often stand for curiosity, and also for intuition. A proportionately *large nose* can indicate we feel that someone is interfering in our lives, whereas a nose that is too *small* may suggest a degree of disinterest.

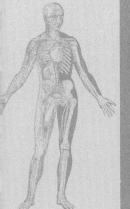
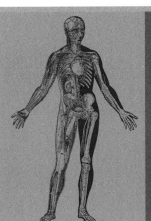

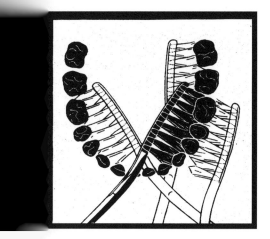

SUBSIDIARY IMAGES AND ASSOCIATIONS

There are four other organs in the body that will often appear in dreams. Interestingly, they can sometimes be represented by machines – the heart being represented by a pump. 'To know in our heart' suggests faith in ourselves; this faith can be symbolized by the shape of a heart. The *heart* is the centre of the being and represents 'feeling' wisdom rather than that of the intellect. It is also representative of compassion, understanding and love, hence the use of its symbolism in romantic poetry. The *kidneys* are organs of elimination, working quietly in the background. To dream specifically of them, therefore, is to be aware of the need for some kind of cleansing in our lives. We may need to eliminate something that is causing us emotional distress.

In Chinese medicine the *liver* is representative of irritability and suppressed anger. Dreaming of our own liver may highlight the life force or our ability to process and make sense of our lives. Again, in Chinese medicine any difficulty with the *lungs* signifies some aspect of grief, and will often manifest in this way in dreams. Spiritually, the *lungs* are the seat of creativity and connect us to our highest Self. Thus, lungs are involved in correct decision-making and, highlighted in dreams, they can represent the Breath of Life – correct action that moves us forward on our Journey of Life.

The *skin* in dreams represents our persona, the part we choose to make visible to other people. It can also represent the protective camouflage we create in order to hide from ourselves. *Damaged, bruised or itchy* skin can suggest emotional hurt. Skin *peeling off* indicates that we may be becoming more vulnerable, or no longer have any need for the protective layer we have built up for ourselves.

For many people *blood* symbolizes the life force and can thus represent our essential energy. Dreaming about blood highlights the need to handle fear connected with loss of life.

We all have need of security and shelter, and freedom from responsibility. The *womb* represents a return to the beginning of physical existence where we are sheltered and nurtured. The *penis* can signify our need to protect our own privacy in an appropriate way. On a slightly more esoteric level, the womb represents our connection with the Great Mother or Mother Earth while the penis suggests the penetrative force of the spirit. *Breasts* in dreams most frequently indicate our connection with the mother-figure and our need for nurturing.

If the *back or backbone* is particularly noticeable in a dream, we should consider the main support structure in our lives. Intellectually, we need to consider our firmness of character.

CLOTHES AND APPEARANCE

Just as costume tells us a great deal about an actor in a play, the clothes and appearance of our dream characters does the same.

THE IMAGERY

It may be the clothes characters wear, it may be the way they wear them; careful consideration usually gives us extra information that is useful in determining the symbolism of clothes in our dream. In dream parlance, various *articles of clothing* have certain symbolic meanings that may well vary according to our culture and upbringing.

Footwear signifies our ability – or otherwise – to be grounded and in touch with everyday life. *Boots* formerly would represent a somewhat mundane attitude, although today they represent safety and warmth. *Lacing up shoes* in a dream was formerly supposed to be a well-known symbol of death or bad luck, as were *shoes on a table*. Nowadays in dreams they are more likely to represent great changes. Acknowledging that shoes we or others are wearing are *unusual* in some way alerts us to the fact that an adjustment needs to be made to our attitude in life.

Any *headgear* tends to acknowledge a person's status in some way. Due regard must be paid to the intellect, and perhaps to wisdom that has been accrued by experience. Particularly if the headgear is *ornate*, our attention in dreams may be being drawn to the character's spiritual powers and their ability to control mundane events. An everyday *workman's cap* may signify that some kind of protection is called for, or that there needs to be submission to a greater authority. We may also need to recognize and respect someone else's beliefs and principles. A *cap belonging to a uniform* suggests that certain standards need to be maintained – those imposed by training and custom.

Outerwear such as *coats* can suggest warmth and love, but also protection. This protection can be either physical or emotional, and particularly in the case of a *cloak*, can suggest spiritual protection or *robes of office* as seen in the Hierophant in the Tarot. Fear of *losing our outerwear* can signify a loss of faith and belief. If the coat is *too short, or not thick enough,* we may be fearful that our love, or

the protection we have, is not adequate for our needs. A *raincoat* also holds the symbolism of protection, but this time against other people's emotional onslaught. *Gloves* would usually represent challenging the status quo, whereas *mittens* suggest covering and protecting oneself.

Nightclothes and *underwear* in dreams suggest a relaxed attitude to life. Additionally, they both can highlight our attitude to self-image and sensuality.

A shirt or formal blouse can suggest appropriate behaviour and actions. A *hair shirt*, however, indicates grief and penitence. We are perhaps aware that we haven't behaved correctly in waking life.

Neckwear of any sort draws attention to our self-expression. *Ties* and other such formal neckwear represent status and respectability. *A scarf*, perhaps being less formal, suggests warmth and a protective influence.

When we, or others, are wearing a *veil or similar article* we are probably trying to hide something. We are only partially accepting knowledge about ourselves or our relationship to others.

THE SIGNIFICANCE

When clothes are particularly noticeable in dreams it will suggest we need to pay particular attention to certain qualities. When *what we as dreamers are wearing* is drawn to our attention it will highlight the façade, or persona, we create for other people. Clothes that *others are wearing* in our dreams can also set the scene for an acting-out of some of the interactions that take place. A *uniformed member of the armed forces*, for instance, might suggest a disciplined approach.

Clothes can often act as a protection against being touched or having the real self violated; they can also conceal or reveal the persona we show others. *Getting undressed* can suggest the shedding of old beliefs and inhibitions. *Losing clothes or being naked* highlights our vulnerability and fears. *Dressing inappropriately,* for example wearing formal clothes on a casual occasion and vice versa, indicates that we are conscious of our own difficulty in 'fitting in' with other people. A man *wearing women's clothing* signifies that we need to be more conscious of our feminine side.

SUBSIDIARY IMAGES AND ASSOCIATIONS

Abnormality in a dream usually represents something that we instinctively feel
is wrong or not balanced properly. If it is extraordinary in the sense of being
completely out of place, such as a nightdress at a formal dinner, it is the oddity of
it that needs to be explored. An awareness of any such digression from the norm
usually alerts us to the fact that we should be paying particular attention to areas in
life that are not in line with the way we feel they should be.

In dreams size is relative. To be especially conscious of size in a dream
highlights how we feel in relation to a person, project or object. *Big* might suggest
important or threatening, whereas *small* might indicate vulnerability or something
'less than' ourselves. Something is noticeably bigger or smaller rather than simply
being big or small. A child learns very early on to make comparisons, and this is
one of the things that we never lose.

To dream of being *fat* alerts us to the defences we use against inadequacy.
Depending on how we think of our bodies in the waking state, we can often
use the dream image of ourselves to change the way we feel. To be *thin* in a
dream might suggest either that we need no defences or that our energy is
somewhat deficient.

To be aware of a *blemish* in a dream is to recognize there is a collection of
negative influences around us that is turning unpleasant or is perhaps even
harmful. *A boil, wart or carbuncle* appearing in a dream is a classic indication that
something has 'got under our skin' in everyday life.

THE WOLF DREAM

Here is a specific example of a dream and how we interpreted the imagery using the Tarot and, in particular, the card of the Moon.

THE IMAGERY

'On a bright, sunny day I was with a group of soldiers (Roman legionnaires, I think) who were marching along a wide country lane.

'I turned a corner so I was in a large field (the soldiers had disappeared) which had a couple of houses and trees on the right-hand side. I was aware of a girl of about seven or eight alongside me. She was what I would call a real "girly-girl" – with a pink dress tied with ribbon at the back and blonde curly hair (not like me at all). She ran on slightly ahead of me and I was suddenly aware of what I thought was a ferocious wolf running towards us. I wasn't frightened for myself, but was concerned that it would attack the girl. However, as the animal got nearer I realized it was the soppiest golden Labrador ever and just wanted to play and have a big fuss made of it.

'By this point, the girl had skipped on ahead and had gone up a path at the top right of the field. I knew this led to her home (one of the houses on the right). The dog and I walked up the path and came upon a small estate of new-build houses (not a style I particularly like). The dog was obviously very familiar with the area, sniffing around the garage and front garden to one of the houses. I knew this was his, and the girl's, home.'

THE SIGNIFICANCE

The main images that are particularly noticeable all have a duality and yet a contrast in them that makes them worthy of interpretation. Contrast and

transformation seem to be the main themes of the dream. There are the Roman soldiers and the new-build housing estate; there is the girl and the dreamer herself – who is incidentally an active participant in the dream, not merely an observer. There is also the 'wolf', which is then recognized as a dog, and a contrast between the field and the housing estate. This duality may initially seem unimportant, but because it has been reinforced in several different ways, it therefore has to be significant.

Part of the resolution of the dream is in the child's and dog's familiarity with the new-build home. The dreamer is shown that something she does not particularly like as an adult can be

acceptable to another, more child-like, aspect of herself. She herself admits that she was never a particularly girly-girl and it is possible that this aspect of her femininity needs to become more developed.

ASSOCIATIONS AND INTERPRETATION

The Roman soldiers probably signify a well-grounded, disciplined approach to life. In turning a corner away from this the dreamer accesses a fresh field. A field often represents the feminine side of one's nature and, following this theme, the dreamer meets a forgotten side of herself, the younger, freer, uninhibited child. Initially, it appears that aspect is threatened by the 'wolf' –

wild untamed energy – but this fear is proved wrong when the gentler, fun-loving side of the dog is revealed. It is worth noting that the adult dreamer is fearful not for herself but for the child.

Interpreting the right turn into the housing estate, the logical, practical side of the personality is highlighted. This perhaps needs some new input, or a newer, more modern way of being rather than the one with the regimented soldiers. Both the child-like side and the animal-loving aspect are at home in this different scenario, suggesting that the dreamer as adult could become accustomed to it.

CLARIFICATION USING TAROT

This dream is useful in that it highlights two different aspects within the dreamer. She had forgotten that a few days previously she had been researching the Tarot cards for a different reason. One of cards she had considered in some detail was the Moon. The dream had presented itself as fresh material and yet contains much of the imagery of the card, particularly in the images of the wolf and the dog and the path leading off into the distance. In the card itself, the crayfish arises from the waters of the subconscious, and in the dream, forgotten aspects of the dreamer's unconscious self make themselves felt, ready for clarification.

This then is an example of the Tarot cards sparking one's Dream Oracle into action which, in this case, presented a personalized version for consideration. It is doubtful that such a dream would have had the same impact without the imagery of the Tarot to help.

EMOTIONS, REACTIONS AND RESPONSES

The way we feel in our dreams, and the way we react to other people in them, can tell us much about how we are perceived. Positive relationships in dreams can underscore the joy we feel in our everyday lives as we enjoy friendship, love and interacting with like-minded people. We can learn about trust in our dealings with others, and about our attitude to sensuality. The converse of this is that conflict situations can appear in our dreams, either physical or emotional, and these can highlight our own negative behaviour, or that of others, or our own vulnerability.

POSITIVE INTERACTIONS AND CELEBRATIONS

Social interactions are a vital part of dream awareness and tell us a great deal about how we ourselves might be perceived.

THE IMAGERY

Positive interactions, sometimes quantified as friendliness, are by and large a deliberate and purposeful action by one character towards another. This might include *kissing* or other physical activity such as *shaking hands; sharing a pleasant activity; helping or being helped by a dream character; giving someone a present or gift; acknowledging someone's presence; having kindly thoughts or feelings about another character.*

Being with other people, whether in a group or otherwise, is often a measure of our maturity and how we handle our public persona. In dreams, a *banquet, party* or any *celebration meal* is a symbol for the joy of being in the company of others like ourselves, and perhaps for mutual nourishment.

Festivals and carnivals were initially a time when the gods and powers of nature were thanked and propitiated in order to ensure a good harvest. In dreams, the important aspect of both secular festivals and carnivals is to suggest that we can drop our inhibitions and allow ourselves the freedom to express ourselves fully. A *holiday* – quite literally, the word means 'holy-day' – is time set apart when we take the opportunity to create space for ourselves and often has this meaning in dreams. To dream of a *public holiday* can indicate that we are part of a more relaxed way of being.

THE SIGNIFICANCE

Behaviour in dreams is highly significant, giving many clues to the way we need to make an interpretation. In the section on Behaviour, Activity and Action (starting on page 157) we looked at more general meanings. Here, we consider specifically positive interactions.

There are two ways to look at what is called positive interaction as part of behaviour in dreams. The first is that instigated by us as dreamer and the second is that initiated by other dream characters. In the first instance, we will wish to interpret our own motives and what we felt. In the second we will look at our own reaction and response to the other's actions.

Using touch as an example, our interpretations will depend on these considerations. *Touch* in dreams suggests making contact. We – or they – are linking with others, usually to our mutual advantage. Touch in a positive way is usually an act of appreciation and approval.

Giving is one of the fundamental needs of the human being; this need is often echoed in dreams. To be able to *share* represents our ability to interact with others, to have others belong within our lives and to assume responsibility for them. *Being given something* in a dream may signify that we are being given information or knowledge, perhaps to share with others and to create an environment that allows for give and take.

SUBSIDIARY IMAGES AND ASSOCIATIONS

As we have seen, festivals, celebrations and occasions for ceremony are psychologically necessary for human beings to be at ease with themselves.

Often, the *maypole* in dreams may be a symbol of one such event – of celebration, of new life and the burgeoning power of nature. When *fireworks* appear in a dream they equally represent celebration in some way. Having much the same significance as an explosion, but in many ways much more controlled, they symbolize our connection with the elemental force of fire.

Any celebrations that mark the passage of time, such as *birthdays* and *jubilees*, *wedding anniversaries* and so on have inherent in them the idea of attainment, of successfully passing a milestone and beginning a new cycle. In today's society they take the place of ancient rites of passage and in dreams will often have this connotation.

When we find we are *attending a party* in a dream, we are often alerted to our social skills – or lack of them. In waking life we may be shy and dislike such gatherings, but in dreams if we are coping with the groups involved, we have a greater awareness of our own sense of belonging. A *pile of presents* in a dream can signify as yet unrecognized talents and skills, while *receiving presents or prizes* suggests that we are being loved and recognized, have overcome our self-imposed obstacles and can be acknowledged for the efforts we have made. We are, in fact, being honoured. The sheer joy of such occasions in dreams will allow the same release of tension that occurs in waking life at such an event. *Laughter* in dreams, as long as we are not an object

of ridicule, has the same significance. *Yelling* in dreams can be an expression of a jointly held enthusiasm, belief or ideal, as with a football or protest chant. Such sound, manifesting a particular resonance, has an impact far beyond that created solely by the individual.

It is recognized that touching is a major form of communication in humans. When such an act appears in dreams it can often signify the transference of power and energy, particularly if the action appears to be in the form of a blessing. *Patting* will be a comfort, as will *hugging*. *Stroking* will tend to indicate the need for healing.

More prosaically, to be *lending someone* an article in a dream will suggest that whatever the article represents is needed only on a temporary basis. If a dream character is *lending us an article*, then we are perhaps not responsible enough to possess what it represents on a full-time basis.

NEGATIVE ACTIONS AND INTERACTIONS

Negativity in dreams is usually related to something that is out of kilter in our waking lives: potential danger, bad behaviour or perhaps emotional issues.

THE IMAGERY

Dreams can often point to a danger in symbolic form, such as *conflict of any sort, fire or flood*. It may be that someone has uncovered a vulnerability within us that we now have an opportunity to deal with, or perhaps that our dreams highlight our own *bad behaviour* or that of others. *Stealing or thieving* is perhaps more of a crime against our emotions than anything else. *Hanging* is a violent act against a person, so if we are present at a hanging in a dream we are being party to aggression in some way and perhaps need to reconsider our actions. If we ourselves are being hanged, we are being warned of some difficulty ahead.

Hitting or punching someone would indicate a level of frustration that is not easily managed in everyday life. *Teasing* in dreams will often arise from an insecurity and an awareness of our own doubts and fears. Teasing can also be a form of *bullying*, of becoming a victim. Pain in any form can become magnified in a dream and be experienced as *torture*. This magnification is designed by the dreaming self to highlight a problem in waking life that needs dealing with immediately.

THE SIGNIFICANCE

Negative actions and interactions are as much an essential aspect of understanding dreams as are positive ones. Any aggressive act is highly threatening to the status quo, and even less obviously negative acts, such as *turning away* from someone, can be meaningful. *Obsessive or repetitive behaviour* in dreams often occurs in order to ensure that we have fully understood the message being conveyed by the unconscious. An emotional difficulty in waking life can be upsetting, and dreams will often highlight this in *chaotic images, highly emotional states, nightmares* and so on. When consideration is given to the theme of the dreams and some kind of order imposed, we are able to begin the process of healing. To *be immobilized* in a dream usually indicates that we have created circumstances around us that are now beginning to entrap us. Often such a dream comes when we are facing the darker side of ourselves – that which could be called 'evil'. A superhuman effort needs to be made to overcome what is holding us down or back.

SUBSIDIARY IMAGES AND ASSOCIATIONS

Unknown impulses or ideas sometimes force us into taking a *defensive attitude* in our dreams. To dream of *being abused* in any way suggests that we have become aware in waking life that we are being taken beyond our comfort zone. *Being attacked* in a dream indicates a fear of being under threat from external events or internal emotions. Hostility is one of those emotions that can be worked through in a dream. If we can identify what it is that is making us feel hostile in a dream, then we can usually draw a parallel in our waking lives and deal with whatever the problem is.

Dreaming of *accidents* highlights anxieties we have with regard to safety or carelessness. To dream of any *weaponry*, including *bullets or guns*, is to be aware of aggression and a desire to hurt. When a *dagger or knife* appears in a dream, the meaning can be either aggressive or defensive. If we are using the dagger to *attack someone* then we may be trying to cut out or alter some part of our personality or trying to get rid of something we do not like.

To experience an article in dreams as having *a fault or being faulty* denotes a negativity or difficulty we may be having in – quite literally – making things work in everyday life. *Exclusion* from any group indicates that certain privileges or aspects of acceptance are being denied us. This can manifest in dreams as a sense of being *punished or rejected*. If we can relate the dream feeling to a situation in waking life then we can deal with the difficulty.

RELATIONSHIPS AND INTIMACY

Dreams can shed light on all aspects of our sensual and sexual natures, on our relationships with others and on our need for contact, both physical and emotional.

THE IMAGERY

One vital stage of growth in a baby's development is its fascination with its own body and the ability to be physical and sensual. This has much to do with how it feels to be in one's own skin, as it were. It is at this point that he or she learns about touch and approval from other people, about whether it is nice to touch or be touched, and even if sensuality is appropriate. This is the growth of *trust*, and in any relationship, whether intimate or otherwise, this is an important part of our awareness of our essential being.

When there is, or has been, difficulty in this area, while any original trauma may be suppressed in waking life, it will often surface in dreams when the time is right for it to be dealt with. Real growth and progress takes place when we are not afraid of the curiosity that allows an innocent exploration of our own bodies and that of others.

One essential aspect of dreaming is the appreciation and feedback we receive from our dream characters. Learning from this interaction, relating to other people in the waking world then runs the whole gamut of relationships, from trusting our own reactions and our ability to communicate, to more intimate behaviour.

Dreams can highlight the whole range of our sexuality. Only if we ignore our own sexual nature and fail to appreciate our own life force do the negative aspects make themselves obvious in dreams. We then become aware of our need for contact and relationship with others.

Within ourselves we hold both masculine and feminine potentials. Various aspects of sex and sexuality can appear in dreams, as much in explanation of our unique drives and

intuition as actual need for intercourse. One potential is always more overt than the other; there is often conflict between the inner and the outer expression of these. This conflict can sometimes show itself in dreams as apparent *bisexuality* and a need for a positive relationship with members of both sexes.

In dreams, *transexualism* and *transvestism* signify a confusion so far as gender roles are concerned. Dreaming of a *hermaphrodite* (someone who is both masculine and feminine) suggests a degree of androgyny – the perfect balance within one person of the masculine and feminine qualities.

Often when there are issues to do with confidence, the image of *castration* will appear in a dream. Its appearance suggests that we fear the loss of drive and masculinity as well as sexual power. To be *castrating someone* suggests an act of disempowerment. Dreaming of *contraception* can indicate

a fear of pregnancy and birth, though interestingly it can equally indicate the choices we make when taking responsibility for our own bodies and actions.

The conflicts that arise in us because of our sexual desire for someone can be dealt with in the dream state through dreaming of *emission, ejaculation* or *orgasm*. *Semen* is a sign of masculinity and of physical maturity and is often represented in dreams by a milky fluid. Dreams actually have an odd way of manifesting images of primitive rites and practices of which we may have no conscious knowledge. Many of these are representations of the sexual act or the spilling of seminal fluid.

In dreams a *kiss* can indicate either a mark of respect or an innate desire to waken that part of us represented by the dream partner. The wish or need to be able to communicate with someone on a very intimate level can also translate itself into *intercourse* in a

dream. Often such an act really marks the integration of a particular part of our own personality.

THE SIGNIFICANCE

Any interaction between dream characters or ourselves as dreamers reflects, to a large extent, our feelings about ourselves and the world we live in. If the characters are *known to us* in waking life or we have a sense in the dream that we *already know them*, then we might learn a great deal about our own reactions by looking at what they do *to* us (passivity), what they do *for* us (positivity), and what the outcome (probability) might be. This gives us an awareness of another part of our personality that can be integrated into our overall persona. Relationship in that sense is not based purely on male/female intimacy, but is – for want of

a better description – the marrying together of two aspects. This is often seen in dreams as an actual *marriage ceremony*.

Sexuality in a dream, in the sense of *feeling desire for someone else* – most often of the opposite sex – is a basic primeval urge for closeness and/or union with what that person represents. We are perhaps searching for a part of ourselves that we have lost. The character to whom we feel linked represents the closest we can get to that part. If we had reached a state of full integration, we would presumably have no need for sexual union with someone else. However, most of us have a desire to be at one with everything that is not part of our own ego.

Such a sensual dream, which highlights the feelings we are capable of having, provides information to enable us to understand our own needs. Sexual activity in waking life might be seen as either the highest expression of love and spirituality, such as with Tantric union, or if purely physically based, entirely selfish. In spiritual terms, each of us is searching for a Mystic Union, a conjoining of all aspects of ourselves, and this will often be depicted in dreams.

Equally, as we mature spiritually we must sometimes undertake tasks and actions that are not always understood by others. If in dreams on our personal journey we find ourselves unpopular, we must decide whether our own code of conduct is right specifically for us or whether, in fact, we are acting for the greater good. Dreaming of being alone highlights being single, isolated or lonely. More positively, it represents the need for independence. As we have said in relation to belonging to a group, loneliness can be experienced as a negative state, whereas being alone is different and can be very positive.

SUBSIDIARY IMAGES AND ASSOCIATIONS

We have written elsewhere of the various interactions possible, both positive and negative, between dream characters. Interactions of intimacy and sexuality do, however, deserve consideration in their own right. Dreaming of an *affair* allows us to release such feelings as a desire for excitement and stimulation, actively seeking emotional satisfaction in a way that we would not usually find acceptable in our waking lives. To dream of *being a bigamist* rather than simply having an affair indicates not being able to decide either between two loves or two courses of action. We are being presented with two alternatives, both of which have equal validity.

Within the human being there is the innate need to make vows, to give promises and above all to symbolize the making of those promises.

Traditionally, the *wedding ring* was a symbol of total encircling love and has this meaning in dreams. Because it is in the shape of a circle, it is complete, with no beginning and no end.

When a woman dreams of being a *bride*, she is often trying to reconcile

her need for a relationship and her need for independence. Dreaming of a *bridegroom* often shows the desire to be more responsible or to take on responsibility for someone else. A *marriage or wedding ceremony* in a dream often indicates the uniting of two particular aspects of our personality that need to come together in order to create a better whole. For instance, our intellect and feelings – or perhaps practical and intuitive sides – may need to be united.

Dreaming of *pregnancy* usually denotes a fairly protracted waiting period being necessary for something, possibly the completion of a project. We may have to be patient and wait for a natural process to take place so that we can fulfil a task. The *umbilical cord* in dreams represents the life-giving force and the connection between mother and child. Severing the umbilical cord often appears in teenage dreams as the child grows into adulthood.

INTEGRAL OBJECTS

Perhaps the most fascinating function of our internal Dream Oracle is the appropriateness of the images it feeds us in our nightly explorations. The smallest objects can be pictured in the minutest detail, drawn from our waking experience, to enhance both the vividness of the experience and our immersion in it. Of course, an object that is misplaced, strangely changed or different in some way, then becomes increasingly important when we look at defining the meaning of the images within our dream.

FURNITURE, FIXTURES AND FITTINGS

Furniture, fixtures and fittings are familiar objects to which we do not pay much attention in real life. However, they need interpretation if they stand out in dreams.

THE IMAGERY

The *computer*, *telephone* and other such *high-technology* images are now such a part of people's lives that it very much depends on other circumstances in the dream as to the correct interpretation of these images. The computer is a tool; it may appear in dreams to signify simply a means to an end. The more we use technology, whether for leisure or personal use, it signifies a widening of the horizons. Just as *books* signify our search for knowledge and the ability to learn from other people's experience and opinions, so technology symbolizes the access we have to a great deal of stored information. The *internet* itself in dreams might represent a source of information, a dispenser of data or purely a means of communication. It

will often depend on our day-to-day use of it as to what particular meaning it has in dreams. Messages from a hidden source or part of ourselves are often brought to us in dreams in a totally logical way, and technological images represent this.

Again, because they are articles used every day, *kitchen utensils* in dreams will have a degree of symbolism. Just as an old-fashioned *cauldron* can be taken to indicate the transformative process, so a more modern *pan* or a *pot* signifies nurturing and caring. Any such receptacle also suggests the containing feminine principle. When a *sieve or colander* is perceived, it is a symbol of our ability to make selections or choices. Perhaps we may be clearing away unnecessary emotion, represented by water draining away, or making

conscious choices that will enable us to extract the best from life.

In dreams, a *light, lamp or lantern* can represent life, guidance and wisdom. An *infrared or heat lamp* has the significance of more modern thinking, whereas a lantern, being more old-fashioned, is likely to represent the past; a *torch* can represent self-confidence. The Hermit in the Tarot demonstrates the idea of a personal light in darkness in his need to be able to move forward despite the darkness around him. The *lamp* can also signify the light of the Divine and immortality. Illumination, wisdom, strength and beauty are all symbolized by a *candle*.

There are certain images that have retained their significance since time immemorial. *Stairs and steps* will always represent stages of ascent, often to a different stage of awareness; a *ladder*, perhaps one that disappears into the sky, suggests how secure we feel in moving from one situation to another, particularly in spiritual awareness. If the *rungs are broken* we can expect difficulty of some kind.

THE SIGNIFICANCE

The furniture that appears in our dreams, particularly if it is drawn to our attention, often shows how we feel about our family and home life, our need for security or stability or conversely the attitudes or habits we have developed. Ordinary everyday articles can represent a range of different attitudes.

A *bed or mattress* can show exactly what is happening in the subtle areas of our close relationships. We can get an insight into how we really feel about intimacy. For some people the bed is a place of sanctuary and rest, where they can be totally alone. *Curtains* and soft furnishings, such as *cushions and pillows*, represent comfort and style and, in dreams, may represent a safe space. To dream of a *pillow fight* indicates a mock conflict without the need for a specific result. Often when *carpets* appear in a dream we are looking at a basic security, our emotional links with finance. *Cupboards and wardrobes* may depict those things we wish to keep hidden, but may also depict how we deal with the different roles we must play in life.

A *table* or desk appearing in a dream is often to do with communal activity, and with our social interaction. As a focus for meeting, whether socially or professionally, it is usually recognized as a symbol of decision-making. A *chair*, depending on what type it is, can indicate that we need a period of rest and recuperation. A functional one, such as an office chair, will suggest that we need to concentrate more on the work in hand.

SUBSIDIARY IMAGES AND ASSOCIATIONS

Because in many ways furniture, fixtures and fittings are subsidiary images to the main theme of our dream, it will be our own personal associations with the article that are the most important. The idea of a

computer being a means of universal communication will be very different for a businessman and a clairvoyant, for instance. For the latter, it might symbolize the Akashic spiritual records and the past, present and future. Even for those who have not yet begun their spiritual journey, communication from spirit may first manifest as though through a computer.

Using the *telephone* suggests a direct one-to-one relationship. Using a *mobile phone or one that is not fixed* suggests a degree of freedom in our communication, though in dreams it can also represent the distractions of the mundane world. Using a *telescope or binoculars* in a dream may mean that we should look at things with both a long- and a short-term view. Without taking account of a long-term view, we may not be successful in the short-term. Conversely, by looking at the long-

term, we may be given information which will help us to 'navigate' our lives in the here and now. Often in dreams a *radio or television* can stand for the voice of authority, or of commonly held ideas and ideals. It may also signify communication from other realms. It is interesting that in waking life people with mental health problems frequently believe they are being communicated with through technology.

Vases and receptacles often symbolize the feminine principle, as may *cups, goblets and chalices*. *Plates and platters* may hold within them the idea of an offering, even if they are just being passed around. *Cutlery* can often represent other 'tools of the trade', and *old-fashioned keepsakes* like love spoons still retain their significance in dreams today.

When *toys* of any sort appear in a dream we may be aware of children

around us, or of our more childlike selves. They will highlight the creative side of ourselves, and the more playful innocent part. Dreaming of a *cricket bat or other such implement* will give an indication of our attitude to controlled aggression, or to how we deal with external forces. Solar and lunar festivals are often symbolized by a *ball* or *balloons*, and the setting free of such objects symbolizes the freedom of the soul. *Board games* appearing in dreams often signify competitiveness or the balance between positive and negative.

FOOD AND DRINK

Food signifies a satisfaction of our needs, whether physical, mental or spiritual. Frequent dreams about eating suggest a hunger for something, not necessarily food itself.

THE IMAGERY

Bread is symbolic of life itself. It is said to be food for the soul and can also represent the need to share, particularly if it appears in dreams in celebratory meals. Depending on whether we are *eating alone or in a group, meals* can indicate acceptance and sociability. When we are *baking* and making cakes it indicates our need to care for others or to nurture an inner, perhaps hidden, need within ourselves. *Cake* itself signifies sensual enjoyment of several sorts. *Sweets and chocolate* in dreams tend to represent sensual pleasures. *Jam* will normally signify an additional sweetness or flavour to life, as does *honey*. In the sense of *preserving fruit* for future use, jam also symbolizes harvesting with awareness. As a healing substance, honey has the power to regenerate the essence of our feelings; more esoterically it symbolizes immortality and rebirth. When *fruits or berries* appear in dreams we are representing in dream form the fruits of our experience or effort, and the potential for prosperity.

As an easily obtainable food, *milk* will always signify nourishment of the inner Self. Physical or worldly satisfaction or needs are often shown in dreams as *meat*, although *raw meat* can supposedly signify impending misfortune. *Fish*, on the other hand, symbolizes temporal and spiritual power. Dreaming of fish connects with the emotional side of ourselves, as well as with our ability to be wise without necessarily being strategic. *Vegetables* represent our basic needs and material satisfaction. They may also symbolize the benefits we gain from the Earth and situations around us. Interestingly, the different layers and facets of our personality are often shown as an *onion*.

THE SIGNIFICANCE

Our need – or enjoyment – of food in waking life fulfils certain psychological needs, and their appearance in dreams will highlight those requirements. Dreaming of *eating* shows that we are attempting to satisfy our basic wants or hunger; it may be that we lack some basic nutrient or feedback in our lives. To *not eat or refuse food* indicates an

avoidance of growth and change. We may be attempting to isolate ourselves from others or be in conflict with ourselves over our body image. *Cooking* can symbolize creativity or nurturing a new skill or ability of any type. To be able to move forward in our lives we may need to blend certain parts of our existence in new and original ways in order to succeed. *Drinking* anything at all in a dream may indicate our need for comfort and sustenance, to be absorbing or taking something in. It symbolizes the interplay between the inner need to sustain life and the external availability of nourishment.

SUBSIDIARY IMAGES AND ASSOCIATIONS

Food and drink have so many associations with pleasure and satisfaction that it is not surprising that the many images linked with them appear in dreams. The *egg*, for instance, is the symbol of unrealized potential, of possibilities yet to come. If in dreams our attention is drawn to the *yolk* – the germ – we must concentrate on which aspects of our everyday life need nurturing or sustaining. Esoterically, the life principle and the germ of all things is said to be contained in the Cosmic Egg.

Bread, because it is made from grain, has always been considered a fit offering for the gods. It was formed into *loaves*, which then became symbols of fertility, nourishment and life. *Manna*, which until recently was thought to be holy bread, is food for the soul and food that is in some way miraculous. *Nuts* were once again reputed to be the food of the gods, and so spiritually enhance the psychic powers; *seeds* epitomize the essential Life Force.

There is a type of euphoria or intoxication that is experienced at certain stages of spiritual development. This usually occurs as we move from one level of awareness to another, and is to do with the sudden influx of new energy. It is said that *grapes* were given to mankind by Dionysius to achieve just such intoxication. An *excess of eating or drinking* in dreams represents an element of overindulgence. Spiritual knowledge that has not been properly assimilated can be represented by *indigestion* in a dream. Recurring dreams are a type of spiritual indigestion that will reoccur until such time as we have understanding.

BURNED BREAD DREAM

This example shows how a specific dream can be interpreted.

THE DREAM

'I was at our local farmers' market. One of the stall-holders in waking life makes the most wonderful sweets, which I usually sample as a special treat. In my dream, he was offering me pieces of burned bread, just as though it were the most normal thing in the world.'

THE INTERPRETATION

Both bread and sweets are symbols of nurturing and caring, the latter to do with the sweetness of life, and the former more relevant to basic nourishment. The burned bread symbolizes the fact that the dreamer's attitude to her basic nourishment is somewhat suspect and not terribly sustaining. As the food is offered by a figure representing the masculine drive in her, she perhaps needs to understand that in fact she does need life to be fun and not made tasteless by over-enthusiasm. Since the theme of the dream is that of sharing, the Tarot card to contemplate would be the Lovers. There is too much inner passion at the moment in the masculine aspect of the dreamer, and a gentler, sweeter approach might be more appropriate.

ARTEFACTS AND SYMBOLIC OBJECTS

There are many small articles that appear in dreams that have a religious, mythological or mystical significance.

THE IMAGERY

One of the most interesting aspects of any oracle is the breadth of inspiration to which it has access. As humans began to evolve from hunter-gatherers, they admired the way that trees grew and saw that *antlers* grew in the same way, so they therefore came to represent power and nobility. As they became more sophisticated they understood that the tools they used, such as the *anvil*, represented a basic force of nature, brute force or a way of creating an initial spark. Since dreams reflect such beliefs, the gods were credited with such powers. The dream symbolism thus became that of forging new life, of creating new beginnings.

Humans used the natural world around them for support, so strange-shaped *stones and natural objects* became talismans and sacred objects to be carried as protection against evil, negative forces or things that were beyond human control. When a move was made into a more philosophical frame of mind, humans began to understand the duality inherent between the spiritual, which could not be seen, and the mundane, which could. They began to comprehend that *heaven* is a state of being where the energy is of such a high frequency that there is no suffering. *Hell* is a state of being where nothing is ever as it seems and could be thought of as continually having to exist in a state of negative illusion. In dreams even today, the polarity of the concept of *heaven and hell* appears when the individual begins to extend his or her awareness into dimensions other than the purely physical or mundane.

THE SIGNIFICANCE

In truth this symbolic imagery may have no explanation other than the fact that we are accessing some really deep knowledge, which often does not appear

until we are quite a way forward on our spiritual journey. They are often *man-made articles*, but have been given special significance in the way that they are used or understood.

The *mystic knot*, for instance, traditionally had no beginning and no end. Its basic meaning suggests an unsolvable enigma and so it has come to represent infinity. The *caduceus*, today a recognized symbol of healing, began life as a representation of the Sanskrit power of life and also of the god Mercury's ability to communicate.

Humans have a deep connection with objects they believe to be sacred. In most pagan religions objects such as stones and drawings were given special powers. In Egypt, the *scarab beetle* assumed significance as it fashioned matter into its own world and thus symbolized the Creator. While consciously we may not believe in this notion, unconsciously we are capable of linking with ancient magic and with the power of belief.

SUBSIDIARY IMAGES AND ASSOCIATIONS

The ancient artefacts of sword, cups, pentacles and wands have already been mentioned in the section on Tarot. In dreams, *cups and chalices* have the same significance as the *Holy Grail*. Mythologically, this was the plate or cup used at

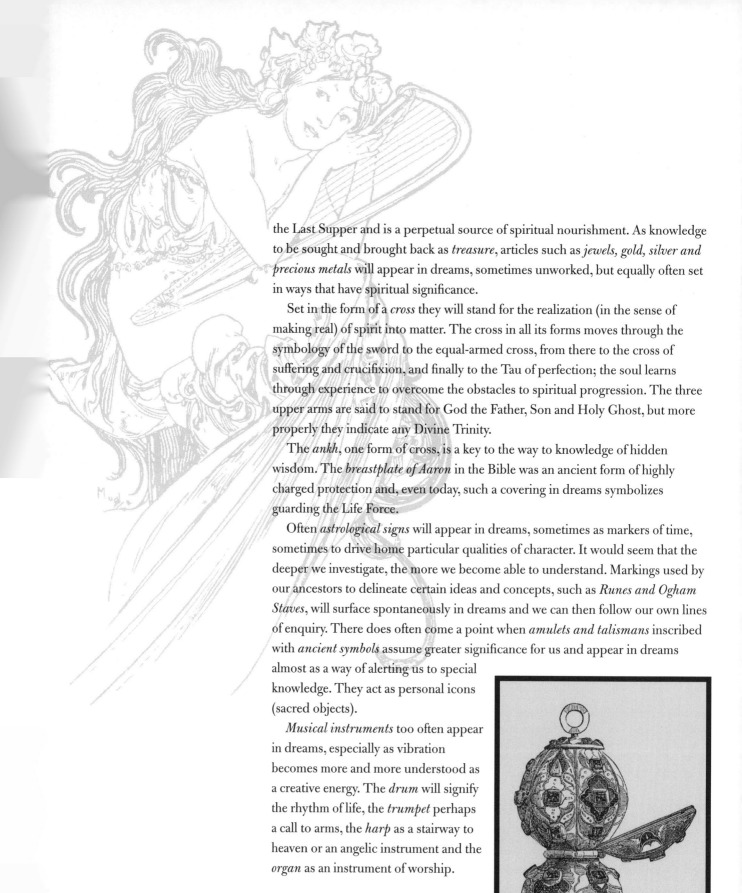

the Last Supper and is a perpetual source of spiritual nourishment. As knowledge to be sought and brought back as *treasure*, articles such as *jewels, gold, silver and precious metals* will appear in dreams, sometimes unworked, but equally often set in ways that have spiritual significance.

Set in the form of a *cross* they will stand for the realization (in the sense of making real) of spirit into matter. The cross in all its forms moves through the symbology of the sword to the equal-armed cross, from there to the cross of suffering and crucifixion, and finally to the Tau of perfection; the soul learns through experience to overcome the obstacles to spiritual progression. The three upper arms are said to stand for God the Father, Son and Holy Ghost, but more properly they indicate any Divine Trinity.

The *ankh*, one form of cross, is a key to the way to knowledge of hidden wisdom. The *breastplate of Aaron* in the Bible was an ancient form of highly charged protection and, even today, such a covering in dreams symbolizes guarding the Life Force.

Often *astrological signs* will appear in dreams, sometimes as markers of time, sometimes to drive home particular qualities of character. It would seem that the deeper we investigate, the more we become able to understand. Markings used by our ancestors to delineate certain ideas and concepts, such as *Runes and Ogham Staves*, will surface spontaneously in dreams and we can then follow our own lines of enquiry. There does often come a point when *amulets and talismans* inscribed with *ancient symbols* assume greater significance for us and appear in dreams almost as a way of alerting us to special knowledge. They act as personal icons (sacred objects).

Musical instruments too often appear in dreams, especially as vibration becomes more and more understood as a creative energy. The *drum* will signify the rhythm of life, the *trumpet* perhaps a call to arms, the *harp* as a stairway to heaven or an angelic instrument and the *organ* as an instrument of worship.

TRANSITIONAL ELEMENTS

Dreams often highlight transition, as though our Dream Oracle is giving us the information we need to understand what has gone before, the situation we are in and sometimes even what we might expect ahead. Those transitions might be rites of passage, such as puberty, or others such as a change of emphasis in the way we work. Often in dreams we envisage ourselves in a particular type of vehicle and can gain much information by some consideration of the type.

THE IMAGERY

The *car* in dreams epitomizes our sense of self. It is a reflection of how we handle life, and the image we wish to project to other people. It also mirrors the physical body, so anything wrong with the car can help alert us to a problem or difficulty. A *lorry* in a dream will generally have much the same meaning as a car, except that the drives and ambitions will be linked more with work and how we relate on a business basis to the outside world. A *commercial van*, for instance, suggests shorter, more intensive periods of activity, whereas something like a *flatbed truck* may represent similar activities of longer duration. Dreaming of an *ambulance* has much the same significance as a lorry. However, it also suggests that professional assistance offered in a timely fashion is available when we are having difficulties in waking life.

A *bus journey* in dreams has a great deal to do with our public image in waking life. It signifies the impetus that enables us to be with other people with whom we share the need to be making progress. A train, being another method of public transport, brings into prominence our attitude to relationships and how we react with others, and clarifies our behaviour in public. A *modern-day train* might suggest a degree of speed and efficiency, while a *steam train* would denote a romanticized, perhaps outdated way of working. An *aeroplane* suggests a swift, easy journey with some attention to detail being necessary.

When a boat is seen in a dream, interpretation of it will depend on what kind it is. Thus a *small rowing boat* would suggest an emotional journey, which requires a great deal of effort. A *yacht* might suggest a similar sort of journey, but one done with some speed, whereas a large ship such as a *cruise liner* would indicate creating new horizons, but in the company of others. On the other hand, a *speedboat* might represent an adventurous spirit, and a canoe a different, personally challenging way of working. Dreaming of a *lifeboat* could indicate our need to be rescued, possibly from our own stupidity or from circumstances beyond our control. Interestingly, it is thought that ships are referred to as 'she' through respect and love. A boat of any sort may therefore in dreams be taken to represent the feminine and the idea of the protective influence as seen in old figureheads.

Imaging independent behaviour, blatant masculinity and daring, the motorbike can also be a symbol of freedom. If in dreams the rider is a woman, the *motorcycle* can suggest an independence of spirit and the ability to blend logic (a masculine quality) and intuition (a feminine one) in order to be ahead of the pack. As a representation of duality, the *bicycle* represents achieving a balance between the physical and the spiritual realms. It also signifies using the correct energy to propel us forward in order to succeed.

A *road or path* in dreams reflects our course of action in everyday life. Any *visible turns* in the road, particularly a blind corner, will suggest some change in direction; a *cul-de-sac* would signify a dead-end or wasted effort. In a dream, *walking for pleasure* suggests a degree of contentment. To be *wandering aimlessly* suggests we need to create goals for ourselves. To be using a *walking stick* is to recognize our need for support and assistance from others.

THE SIGNIFICANCE

We have already seen how important the idea of a journey as a progression towards our own personal goals is. Both the Hero's and the Fool's Journey have given us some very rich imagery. The whole idea of moving between any two points or stages allows us to recognize in dreams just how the Dream Oracle bridges the transitional state between the conscious and the unconscious.

CAMPER VAN DREAM

This example shows how a specific dream can be interpreted.

THE DREAM

'I own a camper van, which is something of a pride and joy. I use it quite frequently as a passport to the freedom of the road. I dreamt I was driving along, when the van ran into some deep water. Next thing I am standing on the bank watching it sink into the water. I panic, but then realize that I can reach into the water and rescue the van. When I pull it out it is the size of a toy. I wake up, and in the main am puzzled.'

THE INTERPRETATION

In waking life the camper van gives the dreamer freedom. Water indicates some strong emotion, and the vehicle we drive often describes our outward persona. There is therefore some emotional trauma around that forces the dreamer to look at his need for freedom from a more objective perspective (being on the safety of the bank). He then realizes in the shrinking of the vehicle that the freedom he craves is not so important after all, but perhaps satisfies a child-like need in him. He perhaps 'plays' at being free.

Interestingly, for this dreamer the card of the Magician would be a suitable one to contemplate. The latter represents learning how to use his tools successfully, but equally to have fun doing so. Manipulation of the circumstances around us to reveal another side of our personality is one such skill.

It often acts as a map so that we may accomplish our transitions successfully. Indeed, a representation of a *bridge* will frequently appear in dreams to draw our attention to this.

The image of a journey becomes more recognizable as time goes on and our dreams achieve greater relevance. Indeed, if we think of our dreams themselves in terms of a journey we can often uncover fresh insights into our motivations and hidden agendas. Many dreams can be considered in this way, quite literally starting off at one point and finishing up somewhere else, the change in environment being necessary to drive home a point.

Often the symbolism of a journey and the transport we use is highly graphic, giving us the opportunity to work out what is holding us back in life. The transport we are using in our dreams, such as the *car*, *aeroplane* or other vehicles, indicates how we are moving through this specific period of our lives. Frequently, as we become more proficient at interpretation, it highlights what is around to help us move forward. The dreaming mind will call on our experiences to date to highlight particular patterns of behaviour, courses of action or recognizable events and environments. We may, for instance, be driving a very utilitarian car rather than a Rolls Royce. Such shifts in perspective can help us to manage our waking lives.

Feelings evoked in the dream by the concept of a journey or of being transported (literally carried across)

can all be successfully incorporated into our interpretations. A sense of anticipation may show we are now capable of moving on confidently, whereas a feeling of dread suggests that we should try to manage our fears better. *Arriving at a destination* shows that we have had some success in what we are attempting to do. Any dream that deals with *departures* of any sort usually suggests new beginnings. When our *destination is known or becomes apparent*, it gives some indication of our conscious ambition and desire.

The whole of the symbolism of driving in dreams is particularly obvious; it represents our basic urges, wants, needs and ambitions. If we ourselves are *driving* in a dream we are usually in control of circumstances around us. We may, however, be aware of our own inadequacies, particularly if we do not drive in everyday life. If we are *overtaking the vehicle in front* we are achieving success, but perhaps somewhat aggressively. When *we are overtaken*, we may feel someone else has got the better of us.

In dreams, if we find that we are a *passenger* in a vehicle, we are probably being carried along by external circumstances in everyday life. Travelling along with *one other passenger* is said to indicate that there may be a beneficial relationship or association on the horizon, while if as drivers we are *carrying passengers* it suggests we may have made ourselves responsible for other people.

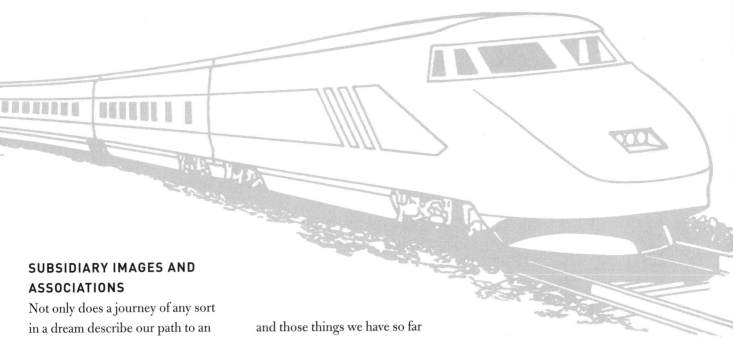

SUBSIDIARY IMAGES AND ASSOCIATIONS

Not only does a journey of any sort in a dream describe our path to an understanding of ourselves in the spiritual sense, it also reflects our everyday lives in a purely practical way. Dreams often show us how we are progressing in life and reveal the joys, personal gains and problems along the way, as we have seen in the Minor Arcana in the Tarot. The *pilgrim's journey*, or rather the idea of a search for a spiritual place, has resonance in the Hero's Journey towards the end of his quest, as also does the Fool in Tarot as he passes through the various stages of learning towards enlightenment.

Arrivals and departures are very obviously transition stages, and *airports, harbours, piers and quays* can all be both points of arrival and points of departure. They can typify in the latter case the beginning of our quest for knowledge and, in the former, our goal achieved. Steps represent changes in awareness, quite literally the steps necessary to succeed. A *tunnel* in a dream usually represents the need to explore our own unconscious

and those things we have so far left untouched.

If we *do not know where we are*, then it is perhaps important that we make an effort to orientate ourselves within a new or unfamiliar environment. If we sense that a *difficult journey is behind us*, then we have come through the problems and pitfalls of the past. To dream of *wanting to leave but not being able to* suggests that there is still some unfinished business we need to complete before we can think about moving on.

To be conscious of the *time of departure* might suggest that we are aware of a time limit or constraint in our everyday lives. Making a *long sea voyage* suggests leaving the known for the unknown, as would *running away to sea* – a more deliberate act of escape. *Disembarking* from such a voyage shows the end of a pet project or period of time, whether successful or otherwise. Actually *escaping* from somewhere in the dream means we are taking steps to gain our freedom, either

emotional or in other respects.

If we *miss* our train, flight or boat, we may be missing an opportunity and do not have the resources immediately available to enable us to succeed. Equally we may feel that external circumstances are imposing an element of unwanted control over us. In terms of transition we may have to wait until circumstances are more in our favour in waking life.

To have *accumulated baggage or to have lost it* suggests in the first case taking on extra responsibility, and in the second that we should look at what we really need to carry us forward. To have *lost our passport or tickets* would indicate that we have not yet given ourselves the go-ahead for something to occur in waking life.

AND THEN I WOKE UP . . .

It is a great deal easier to retain the imagery of dreams when we wake up if we first of all train ourselves to remember our dreams. The dream state alerts us to various ideas and concepts we should be looking at from a conscious perspective, although it may take us a little time to work out exactly what these are and how we can apply them on a personal level. For this reason it is always better to spend some time contemplating our sleep state before we get on with our everyday tasks.

THE IMAGERY

Upon waking, dreamers should take note of exactly how they wake up and how they feel, so have a notebook by the bed to jot down information. Something from the external world may have intruded into the sleeping state, the dream may have reached a natural conclusion or the dream content may have been disturbing enough to shock us into wakefulness. This last occurrence can be either a positive or negative reaction to the content.

If we have been shocked awake, either by an external occurrence or by the content, we can ask ourselves the question 'Had the dream finished?' That way, if the decision is that it has, we can attempt to interpret it as it stands. If it feels as though the dream has not finished then we can consciously run it further forward in our own minds to its natural conclusion. This will help us to discover what might happen next and we can then try to interpret its meaning. If we awoke naturally, aware that the dream had finished, then being able to interpret or validate the dream indicates that our Dream Oracle has achieved its purpose.

At that point, if the message of the dream is not clear, we can again take the dream forward to enhance its meaning, as we saw in the section on Dream Manipulation. This is subtly different from simply allowing the dream to run forward by itself, in that we can look at the content from different perspectives. Firstly we can be 'in' the dream as

dreamer and then manipulate our perspective to see it from our dream character's viewpoint or even from the perspective of dream objects. We may, at this point if we so choose, decide to tie the dream in with one of the Major Arcana illustrations. That way, taking everything into account we can consciously decide the best outcome.

THE SIGNIFICANCE

Rather than dreams being a little world of their own, it has been discovered that every part of a dream has meaning and some relevance to our conscious self. Waking up – a transitional state – is a return to the everyday world and we need to be able to bring back the information given to us. Retaining the dream content and perhaps being able to record our dreams is often helpful when, later on, we look at the various themes that occur as we move forward.

There is a circumstance while sleeping when we become alert to the fact that we are dreaming and that we can wake up. This appears partly as a way of forcing us into taking note of a particular action or circumstance, and partly to enable us to use the therapeutic tool of being able to wake up on demand. This allows us to make an adjustment to a dream that might have a happier ending, as we discussed in the RISC Technique (see page 79).

SUBSIDIARY IMAGES AND ASSOCIATIONS

Our first task on waking is to ask ourselves what relevance the dream has to our everyday lives. It may highlight an issue that has been consciously troubling us or even one that has been lurking around in the background and now needs consideration. By and large, dreams will have a positive content, only throwing up negative imagery to drive a point home. If there does not appear to be relevance to the normal everyday world we might ask ourselves if there is any tie-in to past events or to plans and projects we may have. These latter dreams are not pre-cognitive as such, but may hold clues as to our course of action in the future.

Our second task is to interpret the message as fully as we can and it is here that we draw together the information from each part of the dream and weave it together in a coherent whole. Only when we are certain that we have all the information we need can we file the dream away. We may then, at a later date, wish to carry out some more interpretation on the themes, ideas and concepts that our Dream Oracle chooses for our elucidation.

INDEX

CONCLUSION

W e, like the Fool and the Hero, have come to the end of this particular journey. We have found our inner Dream Oracle, that part of us that knows what is right for us. We have, in a sense, rediscovered the innocent being who had previously been imparting through dreams information that was sometimes understandable and sometimes not. The Oracles of old who spoke in unintelligible riddles needed priests to translate their ramblings; we have learned to be both our own oracle and translator.

We have learned to use the creative altered states of consciousness – from daydreaming to dream manipulation – to focus our minds. These allow our inner being to present the information it has for us as succinctly as possible. In the Tarot, we have used some ancient keys that will open doorways to other mysteries. Finally, we have learned to appreciate the vast source of dream imagery and knowledge that can become available to us if we so desire.

Like children, we have listened to old stories. Like teenagers, we have re-enacted those stories for ourselves and finally, gaining maturity, we have understood why we act as we do. Rather than being something to be feared, dreams and our inner Oracle now remain as mentors and friends to help us on our way into a brilliant future.

Let us then finish with a quotation that expresses the aims of the book:

It is difficult to say what is impossible, for the dream of
yesterday is the hope of today and the reality of tomorrow.
ROBERT H. GODDARD (1882–1945)